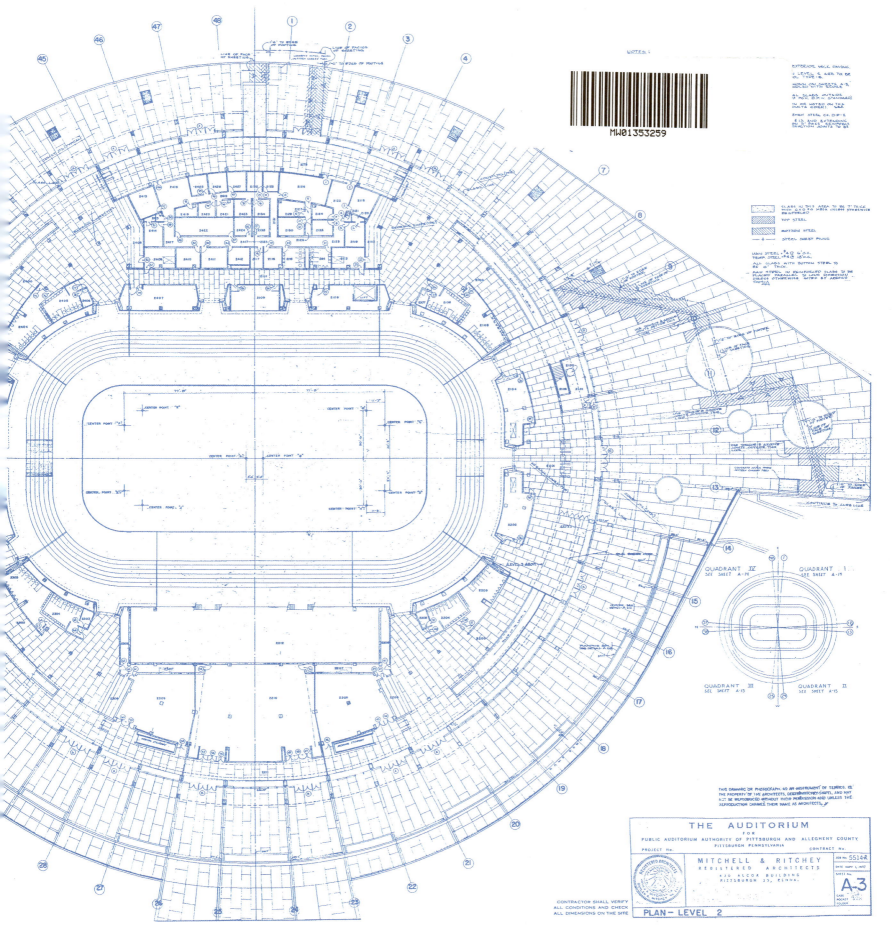

INSIDE THE IGLOO

PITTSBURGH'S FAVORITE GATHERING PLACE

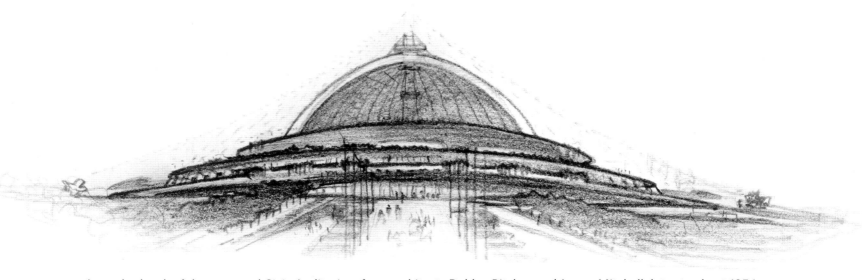

An early sketch of the proposed Civic Auditorium from architects Dahlen Ritchey and James Mitchell dates to about 1956.

CREATIVE DIRECTOR
James M. Kubus

LEAD RESEARCHER/WRITER
Andrew Conte

DESIGNER
Elizabeth Kane Jackson

EDITOR
Sandra Skowron

PROJECT MANAGER
Carol Shrefler

PHOTO EDITORS
Steven Adams
Keith Hodan
J.C. Schisler

CONTRIBUTING EDITORS
Kevin Smith
Sally Quinn

WRITERS
Rege Behe
Jeremy Boren
Alice Carter
Jerry DiPaola
John Grupp
Bob Karlovits
Justin LaBar
Michael Machosky
Joe Rutter
Rick Stouffer

PHOTO TECHNICIAN
Jack Fordyce

GRAPHIC ARTIST
Jason Lanza

COPY EDITORS
Marilyn Anobile
Charles Rondinelli

Copyright © 2010
by Trib Total Media, Inc.

TRIB | TOTAL MEDIA

Pittsburgh Tribune-Review
503 Martindale Street
Pittsburgh, Pennsylvania 15212

Richard M. Scaife Publisher, Inc.

All rights reserved. No part of this book may be reproduced in any form or by any electronic, mechanical or other means, now known or hereafter invented, including xerography, photocopying, recording, or information storage and retrieval systems without permission in writing by the publisher, except by a reviewer who may quote brief passages in a review.

ISBN 978-0-9819589-4-1

'Inside the Igloo' was printed in Pittsburgh, Pennsylvania by Knepper Press

CONTENTS

	foreword	v
	introduction	1
chapter ONE	**Sounds like a plan**	3
chapter TWO	**Going up**	9
chapter THREE	**'In shining pride'**	31
chapter FOUR	**On with the show**	39
chapter FIVE	**Icemen**	45
chapter SIX	**What a sport**	63
chapter SEVEN	**Singing and swinging**	75
chapter EIGHT	**Celebrations**	97
	acknowledgements	105

JAMES M. KUBUS

Andy Masich

KEITH HODAN

FOREWORD
by Andy Masich

AS PITTSBURGH CELEBRATED ITS BICENTENNIAL — commemorating the establishment of Fort Pitt at the forks of the Ohio — the city focused on the modern age.

Civic leaders proudly announced that Pittsburgh was the first city to be powered with atomic energy — from the nuclear power plant in Shippingport, Beaver County — and they laid the cornerstone of the futuristic Civic Arena.

When the arena opened its doors — and roof — in 1961, it was hailed as an architectural marvel that boldly showcased Pittsburgh's rebirth. For the designers and architects who built it, the Civic Arena represented a vision for the future.

The arena development came with a cost unanticipated by its builders. When the substandard housing of the Lower Hill District was cleared for "urban renewal," a vibrant multicultural community was disrupted. Black families in particular were relocated, and a neighborhood rich in culture and jazz tradition was lost.

The arena featured the world's first — and largest — retractable dome roof that allowed audiences to enjoy theater under the stars, a feat praised in magazines and architectural journals throughout the world.

Throughout its history, the arena was a year-round meeting place for Pittsburghers from all walks of life. It hosted everything from the Penguins to the Ice Capades, circuses to wrestling matches and monster truck jams, along with the world's most famous entertainers.

Many Pittsburghers will remember it as Mellon Arena, the name adopted in 1999 and put aside on August 1, 2010, when the naming-rights contract with Bank of New York Mellon expired and the Penguins moved across the street to the state-of-the-art CONSOL Energy Center.

Some will forever picture it as a feature of Pittsburgh's unique skyline.

Many families in the Hill District will remember it as a misdirected public project.

But when its lights go dim and the arena site is redeveloped, Pittsburghers will be caught up in a flood of memories at the passing of an era.

Mr. Masich is the president and chief executive officer of the Senator John Heinz History Center, an affiliate of the Smithsonian Institution and the largest history museum in Pennsylvania; the Western Pennsylvania Sports Museum; Fort Pitt Museum; and Meadowcroft Rockshelter and Historic Village, the oldest site of human habitation in North America, near Avella in Washington County.

FROM ATOP THE DOME OF THE CIVIC ARENA, PITTSBURGH UNFOLDS IN A STUNNING PANORAMA — from the industrial Mon Valley in the southeast, over tree-topped streets of the Hill District and to the low rolling hills above the Ohio River in the west.

The spire of the Allegheny County Courthouse nestles among Renaissance skyscrapers, and the new CONSOL Energy Center rises across the street.

For a half-century, the arena — fondly called The Igloo — has lived at the center of the city's story. Its designers harkened to ancient Rome and Greece to express their ambitions for a space where generations would gather for civil debate and serious sport, for celebrations and thoughtful silence.

With its retractable 4-acre roof of stainless steel, the building proved to the world that Pittsburgh could be not only the brutish plow horse of industry, but home to doctors who cured polio and pioneered organ transplantation, as well as engineers who developed the first computers and put robots in space.

Standing on the west terrace of the half-built arena in 1960, United States Steel executive Bennett S. Chapple Jr. imagined himself among Romans, gazing upon their capital city. He hoped that generations of Pittsburghers might stand at the arena, too, and reflect upon their empire with appreciation for its fiery industrial roots and its modern place as a center for culture, sports, politics and religion.

JAMES M. KUBUS

A MODERN PLACE
by the news staff of the Pittsburgh Tribune-Review

From the Pittsburgh Civic Light Opera's founding in 1946 until its final season in 1958 at Pitt Stadium, rainouts canceled at least 38 shows. Each cancellation could cost as much as $15,000 in rainchecks — a considerable amount in 1946, when individual tickets ranged from 60 cents to $3. CLO ARCHIVES · HEINZ HISTORY CENTER ARCHIVES

SOUNDS LIKE A PLAN
CHAPTER ONE

THE CITY THAT POWERED THE ALLIES TO VICTORY IN WORLD WAR II with steel for tanks, battleships and guns paid a price with dust-thick air and neglect for civic improvements. Department store magnate Edgar Kaufmann Sr. commissioned two local architects in 1947 to come up with a plan.

Radical in their day, the ideas of James Mitchell and Dahlen Ritchey seem commonplace now — because many became reality. Wipe industry from the rivers' confluence for a great grassy park. Build restaurants and condominiums into Mount Washington for the views. Level the Lower Hill District for a sports arena at the center of a vast civic revival.

Meanwhile, the Pittsburgh Civic Light Opera, which performed in the open air at Pitt Stadium, was losing $15,000 in ticket sales every time rain canceled a performance. City Councilman Abraham "Abe" Wolk suggested building a permanent home for the CLO, but Kaufmann wanted to know how it would avoid vagaries of the weather.

According to popular legend, Wolk thought up a solution on the spot: Build a retractable roof, open it on clear, summer nights and close it for rain.

How much would it cost?

Maybe $1 million.

Kaufmann offered to put up half if the city matched his offer.

Making it a reality would take 14 years.

The firm of Mitchell & Ritchey had been hired to work on the arena as well as a new home for the CLO. Early plans for the arena suggested a building with a flat roof for helicopter landings and escalators connecting with Pennsylvania Station. The amphitheater would have a roof made of bat-like, fabric wings coated in plastic resin that could close for bad weather. With a cantilevered roof support, designs evoked Fallingwater, the home Frank Lloyd Wright had built for Kaufmann.

More than two dozen sites were considered for the amphitheater without success, so Mayor David L. Lawrence proposed integrating it into the arena. He and the city's top executives flew out to Palm Springs, California, in 1953 to convince Kaufmann to go along.

When they returned, Pittsburgh had plans for a four-season arena with a retractable steel dome evoking the boundless aspirations of the supersonic age.

The 1949 program for *The Wizard of Oz* gave theatergoers their first look of a proposed amphitheater expected to be ready for the 1950 season.

Arena moments

Construction of the Civic Arena fulfilled a dream of city leaders to build an iconic meeting place that would celebrate the city's emergence from the Industrial Age. Conception to ribbon-cutting took years. Once it opened, the arena hosted everything from musicians and religious revivals to stage shows and hockey. This timeline, which continues throughout the book, highlights important events in the arena's history.

Sept. 16, 1943 Allegheny Conference on Community Development forms, bringing together corporate executives and public officials to lead a Pittsburgh Renaissance of culture, environment and community design.

June 1, 1946 Civic Light Opera opens its first season, at Pitt Stadium, with a performance of Victor Herbert's *Naughty Marietta*. Five shows are rained out in the first season. Pittsburgh Councilman Abe Wolk suggests building an outdoor amphitheater with a retractable roof.

Nov. 18, 1946 Pittsburgh's Urban Redevelopment Authority forms. The agency is given broad powers as the building developer of the Pittsburgh Renaissance.

Oct. 30, 1947 Pittsburgh Regional Planning Association reveals plans for the Lower Hill District. The futuristic proposal includes an arena with rooftop helicopter pad, escalators linking to Pennsylvania Station, nearby apartments and vast open parks.

Dec. 2, 1948 Department store magnate Edgar J. Kaufmann Sr. proposes a $1 million amphitheater with a retractable roof, to be ready for the 1950 CLO season. Kaufmann initially agrees to pay half of the cost, if the city will match his offer.

May 1, 1949 Allegheny Conference makes its first payment, of $1,000, for a flexible amphitheater roof design, entering into a contract with Mitchell & Ritchey architects to design the CLO amphitheater.

July 6, 1949 The Highland Park estate of Robert B. King is considered for the amphitheater, sitting between North Negley Avenue and King Avenue.

Aug. 3, 1949 The Highland Park site is rejected after residents, led by King, file a court injunction seeking to stop construction.

Architects Dahlen Ritchey and James Mitchell; A.H. Burchfield, a vice president of the Civic Light Opera Association; philanthropist Edgar J. Kaufmann Sr. and Councilman Abe Wolk in 1949 examine the proposed "umbrella" amphitheater. CLO ARCHIVES · HEINZ HISTORY CENTER ARCHIVES

THE LOCATION

Highland Park nearly ended up with an amphitheater in 1949 at the estate of Robert B. King near North Negley Avenue.

"Oh, yes, we had quite a battle, quite an argument, there," Governor David L. Lawrence, who had been mayor, said during a 1963 interview. "I thought we had it all solved by going up to the King Estate … and old Mr. King kicked up quite a fuss."

King was an uncle of philanthropist and businessman Richard King "R.K." Mellon, and so Lawrence looked for another site.

The City Planning Commission considered 27 other places, including the Point, Frick Park, the North Side riverfront and Panther Hollow, which called for filling in the valley, which, as an added bonus, would have doubled as an "excellent bomb shelter for thousands of people."

When planners chose Schenley Park, "a big howl went up with the people," Lawrence said.

Fed up by 1953, Lawrence won Edgar J. Kaufmann Sr.'s blessing to combine the amphitheater and arena into one building for the Lower Hill District.

In his 1950 application to the U.S. Patent Office, architect James Mitchell heralded his flexible amphitheater roof as a marvel for bridging the divide between indoor and outdoor venues.

DRS ARCHITECTS INCORPORATED (FORMERLY MITCHELL & RITCHEY)

Edgar J. Kaufmann Sr., the "merchant prince," loved the arts and architecture and had a passion for urban planning and renewal.

He was born November 1, 1885. By 1913, at 28, he was running the family business, Kaufmann's Department Store, Downtown. Between 1913 and 1920, he was said to have tripled the store's sales to $30 million.

Kaufmann used the store to promote the arts and modern design. He became a patron of architect Frank Lloyd Wright, who in 1936 designed for Kaufmann one of the best-known residences ever built: Fallingwater, about 50 miles southeast of Pittsburgh.

Kaufmann was a member of many civic development agencies. In 1947-48, he commissioned Wright to design a civic center for the Point, but it was never built.

Kaufmann died on April 15, 1955. He and his wife, Liliane, are interred at the Bear Run Nature Reserve, which surrounds Fallingwater.

David L. Lawrence (pictured above left) admitted he wasn't a blueprint reader and was unconcerned with building design. He was dedicated to "the work of making things happen."

As Pittsburgh's mayor, head of the dominant Democratic party and chairman of the Urban Redevelopment Authority of Pittsburgh, Lawrence was able to get the business community — most importantly, banker and philanthropist Richard King Mellon — in his corner.

Born June 18, 1889, Lawrence served as Pittsburgh's mayor from 1946 to 1959. During those years, 1,000 acres and 16 major projects had Lawrence's hand on them. About $632 million was spent, including $500 million in private funds. The redevelopment collectively is known as Renaissance I.

Among projects undertaken Downtown were conversion of the railroad warehouse district at the Point into Point State Park and construction of the Gateway Center office complex and the pioneering urban park, Mellon Square.

He served as Pennsylvania governor from 1959 to 1963. Lawrence died November 21, 1966, 17 days after collapsing at a political rally.

Abraham "Abe" Wolk (pictured above right) ran for Pittsburgh City Council in 1937 on a two-plank platform: a summer opera and less smoke.

Born in the Lower Hill District, the son of a peddler, Abe Wolk began practicing law in 1915. Once elected to City Council in 1937, he immediately began pushing for smoke control and for staging operettas on Flagstaff Hill in Schenley Park.

In 1941, he chaired a commission that cited health, destruction of vegetation and the economic impact as reasons to push for air pollution control. He led a delegation to St. Louis to observe its successes. Wolk was instrumental in the founding of the Allegheny County Health Department, the University of Pittsburgh's Graduate School of Public Health and the Pittsburgh Civic Light Opera.

He was an early proponent with his friend Edgar J. Kaufmann Sr. of a new civic amphitheater with a removable roof.

He left City Council in 1956 to become an Allegheny County judge.

Wolk retired to Sarasota, Florida, where he died in 1983.

ALUMINUM VS. STEEL

Once a location was finalized for Pittsburgh's new arena, the battle began: Which of the city's metals producers, United States Steel Corporation or the Aluminum Company of America — Alcoa — would supply product for the dome?

The use of aluminum or steel as structural materials is a decades-long competition worldwide. The proposed arena was the world's first retractable dome and, at 417 feet, the world's largest dome, a title it held until the opening of the Houston Astrodome in 1965.

Alcoa appeared to have the inside track. Using an aluminum "skin" cost about $242,000 less than stainless steel — $647,836 versus $889,836, respectively. Aluminum for a few dollars more was available in colors, including gold, green and gray.

Physics is believed to have factored into the final decision. Stainless steel won out because aluminum's expansion properties when heated were too great and because stainless was believed to be easier to maintain.

About 166,000 square feet of stainless steel sheeting was placed atop the arena, supplied by United States Steel, Allegheny Ludlum Steel Corporation, Crucible Steel Company and Jones & Laughlin Steel Corporation. Pittsburgh's Limbach Company fabricated it in trapezoidal shapes ranging in width from 30 inches to 13 feet.

Set designer Harold Helvenston shows off the lifting stage area inside a model of the proposed Civic Auditorium on April 16, 1959, while the arena was under construction.

DRS ARCHITECTS INCORPORATED (FORMERLY MITCHELL & RITCHEY)

Aug. 18, 1949 Panther Hollow — between Carnegie Institute of Technology and the Carnegie Museums — is considered for the amphitheater. Planners say it could double as a bomb shelter. The proposal is rejected.

Feb. 1, 1950 Edgar J. Kaufmann Sr. unveils plans for a CLO amphitheater with 10,500 seats and motorized, bat-like wings for a roof. He pledges another $500,000 for the project.

Feb. 2, 1950 Pittsburgh Planning Commission considers other amphitheater sites: North Shore, the Point, Schenley Park.

May 27, 1950 The planning commission selects Schenley Park on a site near the Schenley Oval. The public objects, and the plan is dropped.

Sept. 19, 1950 Planning commission declares 91 acres of the Lower Hill "blighted," allowing the city to take properties by eminent domain for demolition. A city report finds that 60 percent of dwellings need major repairs or lack a private indoor bathroom.

Aug. 1, 1952 Allegheny Conference enters into contract with Mitchell & Ritchey to design a site plan for the Lower Hill.

Jan. 19, 1953 Mayor David L. Lawrence wins Kaufmann's approval to combine the arena and CLO amphitheater into one Lower Hill project after flying to Kaufmann's winter home in Palm Springs, California, aboard the private plane of General Brehon B. Somervell, Koppers Company board chairman and president of the CLO.

Feb. 26, 1953 The Allegheny Conference unveils plans to develop 106 acres of the Lower Hill with not only a municipal arena for CLO and sports, but also a grand opera house, a playhouse and apartments.

May 1, 1953 Lawrence asks City Council to accept Kaufmann's $1 million gift, calling it a "splendid start for the erection of a magnificent and unique public facility."

Oct. 28, 1953 The Public Auditorium Authority of Pittsburgh and Allegheny County forms. The authority will lead the construction and own the auditorium.

April 29, 1954 Lawrence signs a City Council proclamation, accepting a $1 million gift from the Edgar J. Kaufmann Charitable Trust. The city and county each agree to pay $1.5 million. The balance of the estimated $11 million cost will come from corporate contributions and a public bond issue.

"A city — a great city — must have some place for its people to assemble. Television, with all its wonders and its errors, is not a complete substitute for flesh and blood. To keep the city in the human scale, this central meeting place is part of our urban design. In my judgment, the redevelopment of the Lower Hill — a giant bite from the core of the city — will be the greatest of our Pittsburgh projects, under way or yet envisioned."

— David L. Lawrence, in his address to Harvard University's Graduate School of Design, May 1956.

Wrecking company owner Robert J. Omslaer directs James Follin of the U.S. Urban Renewal Commission; Pittsburgh Mayor David L. Lawrence; Arthur B. Van Buskirk of the Allegheny Conference on Community Development and William R. Davlin, state secretary of commerce, in the May 31, 1956, ceremonial start of the arena project.

UNIVERSITY OF PITTSBURGH

GOING UP
CHAPTER TWO

GRASPING A CROW BAR WRAPPED IN FESTIVE RIBBONS, MAYOR DAVID L. LAWRENCE PRIED THE FRONT DOOR FRAME from a red brick, two-and-a-half story house at 1206 Epiphany Street in the Lower Hill District. Moments later, the real demolition of the building started, and Pittsburgh's most sweeping urban renewal project had begun.

HEINZ HISTORY CENTER ARCHIVES

From that last day of May in 1956, bulldozers razed 1,000 buildings — homes, shops, churches and synagogues — more than 80 city blocks. About 1,500 families, two-thirds of them black, were forced to find new homes. In all, the project cost $22 million with state and federal help. Adjusted for inflation, it would have cost roughly $156 million today.

Banker Thomas Mellon first developed the Hill more than 100 years earlier, buying up farmland and dividing it into parcels. His former home, at 9 Wylie Avenue, was among those leveled.

Lawrence had been committed to tearing down the Lower Hill. Political leaders called it the city's worst slum with open sewers and many outhouses. Three-quarters of the dwellings were deemed substandard, and the death rate was 32 percent higher than the rest of the city.

City leaders hoped to create space for not only an arena, but for apartments designed by the famous architect I.M. Pei, the Crosstown Boulevard, office buildings and a center for the arts.

"Our marvel, the first of its kind in the world, will replace a slum where men and women now live in misery and degradation," said civic leader Leland Hazard, a vice president and director of Pittsburgh Plate Glass Company, during a 1953 ceremony to present the proposal.

A steam shovel broke ground for the arena in April 1958. Construction — starting with a massive excavation of clay, shale and old foundations — would last three years.

As for the rest of the plan: Only the first phase of Pei's apartment complex opened, as the Washington Plaza apartments; Chatham Center broke ground in 1964; and plans for a world-class symphony hall in the upper parking lot above the arena fell apart over cost concerns.

HEINZ HISTORY CENTER ARCHIVES

Sept. 12, 1955 The Federal Housing and Home Finance Agency promises $17.4 million in loans and grants for redeveloping the Lower Hill.

Jan. 8, 1956 Mayor David L. Lawrence says in a State of the City speech that the Lower Hill will be razed within five years, relocating 1,800 families.

Feb. 4, 1956 Hockey News announces a new Pittsburgh arena.

March 26, 1956 URA begins buying Lower Hill properties, starting at 4 Pride Street.

May 31, 1956 Demolition of Lower Hill begins at 1206 Epiphany Street.

April 25, 1958 Arena construction starts with a steam shovel digging the first scoops of dirt. Workers need to remove 300,000 cubic yards of clay, shale and old foundations.

Oct. 29, 1958 Concrete is poured for the auditorium. The foundation includes 1,500 linear feet of tunnels.

April 13, 1959 First section of cantilever arm placed. Fabricated at United States Steel's American Bridge Division, the completed arm will extend 205 feet to hold up the arena's eight roof leaves.

May 30, 1959 The CLO raises the Melody Tent — a temporary, orange-and-green home near the arena construction site — opening with *The Most Happy Fella*. In a 1955 report to stakeholders, CLO Executive Secretary Edward H. Young said the CLO could not afford costly rainouts and needed a temporary home until the new arena opened.

Oct. 1, 1960 Demolition of St. Peter the Apostle Catholic Church, an Italian nationality parish on Fernando Street, begins. Parishioners had sent 30,000 postcards to the mayor to save the church and a plea to Pope Pius XII, asking him to intercede.

Dec. 22, 1960 Pittsburgh Progress, an arena-opening gala, is canceled after a 21-day workers' strike. The weeklong event would have included three days of symposiums on metropolitan planning, culture, education, health, transportation and other contemporary issues.

Aug. 26, 1961 Melody Tent holds the final CLO performance, *Destry Rides Again*.

Sept. 17, 1961 The Civic Arena opens with a ribbon-cutting ceremony. Many among the 5,000 initial visitors marveled at the retractable roof — and complained about the lack of public water fountains inside the arena.

The Lower Hill District had been the center of the universe for so many people.

Bill Blakey's cousin, Art, became a famous jazz drummer playing clubs and restaurants there. Every major black musician and entertainer, it seemed, went to the intersection of Centre Avenue and Fulton Street to play at the Bamboola Club, Stanley's or the Washington Club.

Immigrants came from Greece, Poland and Lebanon. Walter Samreny ran a famous Syrian restaurant on Webster Avenue, blocks from where Muzio Frediani sat at a Linotype machine to print the Unione, the nation's oldest Italian weekly newspaper.

The city's oldest Jewish congregation, Beth Hamedrash Hagodol, made its home in the neighborhood and lost it to the wrecking ball. The African Methodist Church at 1200 Wylie Avenue fell to progress. St. Peter the Apostle Catholic Church on Fernando Street did, too — even after parishioners sent 30,000 postcards to the mayor's office and pleaded for help from Pope Pius XII.

A half-dozen mayors came out of the Lower Hill, including Mayor Sophie Masloff, the only woman to hold the job. She was raised on Roberts Street. Councilman Abe Wolk grew up there, too.

Living conditions, especially for blacks, improved over the second half of the 20th century, yet former residents of the Lower Hill say the camaraderie of people from different races and ethnic backgrounds has never been matched.

"Everything is better," Blakey says, looking back. "One thousand times better — but still not as good."

Bandleader Will Hitchcock plays the trombone with his Dreamband at the Harlem Casino at Roberts Street and Centre Avenue during the 1930s and 1940s. TEENIE HARRIS · CARNEGIE MUSEUM OF ART

Businesses line Wylie Avenue in the Lower Hill, near Fullerton Street, in October 1956. This part of Wylie Avenue, along with Fullerton Street, was taken by the Civic Arena project. Downtown is in the distance.

Hazel and Shomin streets in the Lower Hill looking southeast onto Shomin Street, about October 1956. Both streets disappeared with the Civic Arena project.

HEINZ HISTORY CENTER ARCHIVES

HILL FACTS

» The first home razed in the Lower Hill District, at 1206 Epiphany Street, was one of three owned by Rachel Friedman with a combined worth of $3,640.

» A neighborhood survey in 1950 found that rates of tuberculosis and people on public assistance were three times higher in the Lower Hill than in the rest of the city.

» Nearly 1,900 families had to be moved from the Lower Hill: 1,265 nonwhite and 620 white. Of them, 975 nonwhite families and 367 white ones were eligible for public housing.

» "It is our hope and our belief that the redevelopment of the Lower Hill will result in improved housing standards for almost all of its present residents." — Urban Redevelopment Authority report to City Council on June 7, 1955.

» For the demolition of the Lower Hill District, the city's Urban Redevelopment Authority agreed to spend $14.4 million buying properties and $4.1 million tearing them down. It expected to make back $9 million by selling the land to developers, and it used federal, state and city grants to cover the remaining costs.

» The site for the arena required the purchase of 205 parcels. The overall project required 752 parcels.

Workers from the Wheel and Axle Division of United States Steel's Homestead Works measure steel wheels for the retractable domed roof of the Civic Arena. The dome contains more than 3,000 tons of Pittsburgh steel including the wheels pictured in this September 1958 photo.

WILLIAM J. GAUGHAN COLLECTION, AIS.1994.03, ARCHIVES SERVICE CENTER, UNIVERSITY OF PITTSBURGH

November 14, 1958   DRS ARCHITECTS INCORPORATED (FORMERLY MITCHELL & RITCHEY)

April 1959   DRS ARCHITECTS INCORPORATED (FORMERLY MITCHELL & RITCHEY)

April 1959   DRS ARCHITECTS INCORPORATED (FORMERLY MITCHELL & RITCHEY)

April 1959
DRS ARCHITECTS INCORPORATED (FORMERLY MITCHELL & RITCHEY)

DRS ARCHITECTS
INCORPORATED
(FORMERLY MITCHELL
& RITCHEY)

Civic Light Opera Melody Tent performances

The orange-and-green Melody Tent went up at the Civic Arena site to host Pittsburgh Civic Light Opera productions while the arena was under construction. The tent housed 23 shows.

1959
The Most Happy Fella June 15-27
The Student Prince June 29-July 4
Li'l Abner July 6-18
Rosalinda July 20-25
Bells Are Ringing July 27-August 8
Naughty Marietta August 10-15
Say, Darling August 17-29
Guys and Dolls August 31-September 5

1960
The King and I July 8-14
Annie Get Your Gun July 4-9
Show Boat July 11-16
Kismet July 18-23
The Pajama Game July 25-30
Brigadoon August 1-6
Rose Marie August 8-13
South Pacific August 15-27

1961
Calamity Jane July 3-8
Show Girl July 10-15
The Chocolate Soldier July 17-22
Take Me Along July 24-29
Damn Yankees July 31-August 12
Kiss Me, Kate August 14-19
Destry Rides Again August 21-26

April 18, 1960

April 18, 1960

May 4, 1960

Fall 1959 PHOTOS: DRS ARCHITECTS INCORPORATED (FORMERLY MITCHELL & RITCHEY)

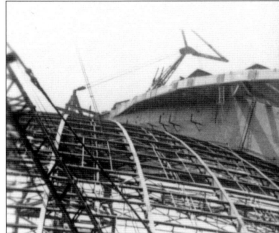

May 4, 1960

June 16, 1960

June 16, 1960

Workers construct the arena dome, which rises to the height of a 12-story building. More than 3,000 tons of structural steel hold up the dome, which is topped by a stainless steel skin weighing 180 tons.

CARNEGIE MELLON UNIVERSITY ARCHITECTURE ARCHIVES

Sept. 19, 1961 The Ice Capades opens the arena with 13 shows. Inspired by the Ziegfeld Follies, Pittsburgher John Harris came up with the idea for an ice show in 1936 as a way to draw more fans to watch his hockey team at the Duquesne Gardens.

Oct. 14, 1961 The Pittsburgh Hornets play their first American Hockey League game at the arena. The team had disbanded in 1956 when the Duquesne Gardens was torn down. It returned at the new arena as a farm team for the Detroit Red Wings.

Oct. 17, 1961 The first wrestling show features Buddy Rogers, Johnny Valentine, Crusher Lisowski and Haystacks Calhoun.

Oct. 19, 1961 The first concert features Judy Garland.

Nov. 5, 1961 The Rens play their first American Basketball League game. The team lasted just two years but featured Connie Hawkins, a Brooklyn playground legend who went on to play in the National Basketball Association and entered the Basketball Hall of Fame.

Nov. 7, 1961 The Harlem Globetrotters appear at the arena for the first time.

Dec. 6, 1961 The first college basketball games feature Duquesne University over Carnegie Tech, 78-40, and Ohio State University over University of Pittsburgh, 99-79.

June 21, 1962 Construction starts on Washington Plaza, the first of three proposed apartment towers. The other towers were never built.

July 2, 1962 The CLO opens its first arena event, the *Carol Burnett Revue*.

Nov. 20, 1962 Ringling Bros. and Barnum & Bailey Circus appears at the arena for the first time.

Dec. 7, 1962 Sammy Davis Jr. performs. He was a member of the famous Rat Pack that included Dean Martin and Frank Sinatra.

Jan. 24, 1963 Boxer Cassius Clay, who later changes his name to Muhammad Ali, knocks out Charlie Powell in the third round.

Sept. 2, 1963 The Roman Catholic Diocese of Pittsburgh says Labor Day Mass.

Sept. 15, 1963 The New York Philharmonic, conducted by Leonard Bernstein, performs. He vows to never return, complaining about the acoustics.

Oct. 3, 1963 The Perry Como NBC-TV Spectacular broadcasts from the arena. Como is a native of Canonsburg in Washington County.

August 15, 1960 CARNEGIE MELLON UNIVERSITY ARCHITECTURE ARCHIVES

November 7, 1960 CARNEGIE MELLON UNIVERSITY ARCHITECTURE ARCHIVES

c. 1960
DRS ARCHITECTS INCORPORATED (FORMERLY MITCHELL & RITCHEY)

December 1960 CLYDE HARE ARCHIVE

1960 CARNEGIE MELLON UNIVERSITY ARCHITECTURE ARCHIVES

1960 CARNEGIE MELLON UNIVERSITY ARCHITECTURE ARCHIVES

25

August 1961 CARNEGIE MELLON UNIVERSITY ARCHITECTURE ARCHIVES

August 1961 (above and right)
DRS ARCHITECTS INCORPORATED (FORMERLY MITCHELL & RITCHEY)

September 1961 DRS ARCHITECTS INCORPORATED (FORMERLY MITCHELL & RITCHEY)

September 1961
DRS ARCHITECTS INCORPORATED
(FORMERLY MITCHELL & RITCHEY)

The stainless steel skin of the arena dome takes on a semi-transparent look in a time-lapse photo taken over two and a half minutes — the time needed to open the retractable roof.

DRS ARCHITECTS INCORPORATED (FORMERLY MITCHELL & RITCHEY)

'IN SHINING PRIDE'
CHAPTER THREE

IT SEEMED ALL THE WORLD CAME TO THE LOWER HILL DISTRICT ON THE AFTERNOON OF SEPTEMBER 17, 1961. As the Pittsburgh Symphony Orchestra played *The Star Spangled Banner*, the stainless steel dome opened and a shaft of sunlight shot through, cutting across the musicians on the floor below. An attorney for the Allegheny Conference on Community Development sobbed, overcome by the moment.

The grand opening of the arena represented a monumental shift for the city from its industrial past as it drew dignitaries, entertainers and reporters from around the world to marvel at its engineering: The structure rises to the height of a 12-story building without a single interior support, hanging instead from a 260-foot steel cantilever arm.

What really shocked the world was that it could happen in Pittsburgh.

"If one of the drabbest and dirtiest of cities has been able to remake itself in shining pride. Any city in the U.S. should be able to follow its example," Fortune magazine declared in a 1961 story on the arena.

Originally, the arena would have opened in June of 1961 with a week-long celebration called Pittsburgh Progress. Great minds on city planning, architecture, science and culture would have gathered: Dr. Jonas Salk would have talked about medical breakthroughs like his polio vaccine, and David Rockefeller would have come from New York to discuss banking.

As it turned out, Pittsburgh had not progressed as far as organizers might have hoped. The event was canceled when labor strikes delayed the grand opening by three months.

INVITATION AND PHOTO OPPOSITE: CARNEGIE MELLON UNIVERSITY ARCHITECTURE ARCHIVES

A BETTER FIT

In 1957, before the arena opened, officials called it the Civic Auditorium Amphitheater — a nod to the building's dual purposes.

After it opened in 1961, city sign makers decided that Civic Arena fit better on street signs. Another popular choice was The Pittsburgh Dome, but that never stuck.

By April 1988, city Councilman Mark Pollock suggested renaming it the Richard S. Caliguiri Arena, for the city's popular mayor who had been diagnosed with a rare protein disorder called amyloidosis. Caliguiri died a month later.

Allegheny County Commissioner Pete Flaherty saw marketing potential in officially naming it "The Igloo" in 1992.

Five years later, the Penguins sold the name, Allegheny Energy Dome, for $5 million to a power company. The problem was that the team did not own the arena or the rights to the name. That changed when the Penguins declared bankruptcy, and a federal judge awarded the arena's naming rights to Mario Lemieux, who took over the team.

The Penguins sold the name to Mellon Financial Corporation in December 1999 for $18 million over 10 years. Even after Mellon sold its retail banking operations two years later and changed to Bank of New York Mellon, the arena kept the Mellon name.

The name reverted to Civic Arena on August 1, 2010, when the Penguins left for the brand-new CONSOL Energy Center.

The arena opened with a ribbon-cutting on September 17, 1961. From left: United Steelworkers President David J. McDonald; former Pittsburgh Mayor, then-Pennsylvania Governor David L. Lawrence; former city Councilman, then-Allegheny County Judge Abe Wolk; Allegheny County Commissioner William D. McClelland; Public Auditorium Authority Chairman William B. McFall and Pittsburgh Mayor Joseph M. Barr. CLO ARCHIVES · HEINZ HISTORY CENTER ARCHIVES

The arena's exhibit hall once housed car shows and exhibits for local trade expositions but in later years the space was converted into storage, the auxiliary press area for playoff games, a carpentry shop and an area for repairing worn-out arena seats. Rows of broken seats were stacked on shelves around a center table, where workers cannibalized old parts to make repairs. MELLON ARENA

ENGINEERING MARVEL

Dimensions The arena is actually an oval — 403 feet across one way, and 417 feet in the other — and stands 136 feet high, or as tall as a 12-story building.

Leaves The roof is divided into eight 45-degree sections, six movable and two stationary. Moving at four feet per second, the leaves open in two and a half minutes. Four of the six movable leaves are mounted on 12 wheels each, while the remaining two leaves have fewer wheels. The leaves taper in about six inches for every 15 feet of height. Each leaf weighs about 300 tons.

Bearings Each movable leaf swivels on a spherical bearing, 21 inches in diameter and weighing 1,000 pounds. Machined from stainless steel, the bearings are polished to a mirror-like finish to reduce friction.

Motors Each movable leaf has five motors and brakes. The two top leaves have five 25-horsepower electric motors; the intermediate leaves have 20-horsepower motors; and the lower leaves have 10-horsepower motors.

Steel About 3,000 tons of structural steel went into the roof.

Stainless steel The stainless steel dome consists of 7,800 pieces, ranging from 30 inches to 13 feet in width.

Aluminum Bidders competed to cover the dome in aluminum, with a gray aluminite surface, a gold-colored anodized look or one with a green Alodine treatment. Designers chose stainless steel because of its lasting attractiveness, weather resistance, strength, maintenance ease and durability.

Interior of the dome Ceiling panels are steel with a baked enamel finish, perforated to absorb sounds into a 3-inch acoustic fiberglass blanket inside.

Foundation Before starting construction, crews removed 350,000 cubic yards of clay, shale and old foundations.

Basement The bottom ring of the arena includes 1,500 feet of tunnels to bring fresh air into the building while housing plumbing and electrical conduits.

A crow's nest inside the roof of the arena, sits high above the rink. It's about 20 feet square with steel pipes that serve as railings. Workers must climb more than 100 metal stairs to get there. The stairway along the spine of the building has the feel of a submarine corridor with steel walls covered in 1-inch rivets. Steel beams are stamped with the symbol for United States Steel. The passageway follows the curve of the building, eliminating the feeling of climbing. On the way down, the walkway appears to go up because of the curve.
JAMES M. KUBUS

The special-effects crew from the movie *Sudden Death* are among the visitors who have left their mark inside the crow's nest.
JAMES M. KUBUS

THE HIDDEN AREAS

» Scheduling arena events from tractor pulls to circuses to rock concerts and hockey games can require the flexibility and choreographic skills of a dancer. Employees of arena operator SMG worked in the arena's old ballet warmup room laid beneath the gray speckled carpet. The old hardwood flooring could be heard when someone walked across the floor.

» What do they make in the carpentry shop? "You name it, we're doing it," said General Manager Jay Roberts with SMG, the arena operator. That includes breakable props for wrestling shows so the performers have something to throw at each other.

» In the bottom ring of the arena, a 10-foot-wide concrete walkway collects water that runs into drains in the floor and allows air to enter into the HVAC system. The ring runs under the bottom of the building and holds rows of pipes for sewage, water and electric conduits.

» The arena's original loading dock has been turned into "Ye Olde Garden Shoppe," as workers have written in paint on the back wall. It holds garden hoses, shovels and other landscaping equipment. The garage was too small for the large equipment trucks that most performers now use.

» It seems almost every Pittsburgher has some memory of the last time the arena roof was opened. Roberts says it was opened in 1993 for a WWE event that featured fireworks. It was opened all of the summer of 1994 during renovations to add luxury boxes on the upper levels. It opened the summer of 1995 for filming of the movie *Sudden Death*. Roberts said the roof was opened all the way in 1997 for maintenance and it was partially opened in 1998 and 1999, again, for maintenance. It hasn't been opened since.

» Inside the crow's nest: Every time a kid lets go of a balloon, it ends up here. The view drops right to the rink. Among the visitors signing the center panel are Penguins right winger Eric Godard.

» True to the arena's Space Age roots, engineers could operate the building from a 20-foot-long Supervisory Data Center that looked as if it came directly out of NASA's Johnson Space Center. With dials, knobs and flashing lights, the units sat in the mechanical room and allowed workers to operate generators, chillers, compressors, fans and lights from one central panel.

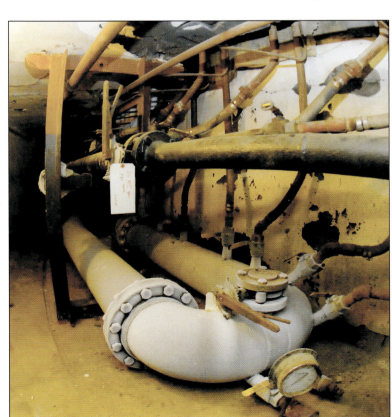

Behind a row of pipes that runs through the lowest level of the arena, a narrow corridor leads to a 5-foot-high wooden door that looks as if it came off an old-fashioned ice box. Inside the small room are pipes coated in tiny ice crystals. A note hangs from a large valve, tied on like a toe tag with a message written in red marker: "Do not open. Pipe leaks." The chilling pipes beneath the ice run across the short length of the rink. At the CONSOL Energy Center, as at all new arenas, the pipes run the length of the rink. The longer the pipes are, the cheaper and easier they are to maintain.
JAMES M. KUBUS

Oct. 23, 1963 The Moscow State Circus opens the first of 10 shows over eight days.

May 2, 1964 Eight hundred protesters kneel in prayer outside arena during the General Conference of the Methodist Church, opposing racial segregation.

Sept. 14, 1964 The Beatles make their only arena appearance, with 4,000 fans greeting them at the airport and 12,500 of them screaming through the performance.

Oct. 21, 1964 Construction starts on Chatham Center. From a penthouse in the Mellon-U.S. Steel Building, Richard K. Mellon presses a button that sets off fireworks, including some that simulate the outlines of the planned 19-story office building and hotel, billed as a "city within a city."

April 9, 1965 The arena loses the title of "world's largest dome" when the Houston Astrodome opens.

Sept. 1, 1965 The Beach Boys

Nov. 24, 1965 The Rolling Stones perform, the first of at least five concerts through 2003.

April 11, 1966 James Brown, the "Godfather of Soul," makes his first of at least 11 arena appearances.

April 23, 1966 Bob Hope has a benefit show.

Oct. 14, 1966 Harry Belafonte

Feb. 3, 1967 The Supremes draw a crowd of 12,329, among the largest to date.

Feb. 14, 1967 Bill Cosby

April 22, 1967 Righteous Brothers

April 30, 1967 The Hornets win the Calder Cup in the final American Hockey League game. When Billy Harris scores 26 seconds into overtime, it is the final goal in the franchise's history.

May 17, 1967 The American Baptist Convention opens.

July 2, 1967 Frank Sinatra plays the first of eight performances at the arena. Backstage, Ol' Blue Eyes insists on drinking tea from a china cup, sending an arena official scurrying down to Kaufmann's department store to fulfill the request.

Oct. 11, 1967 The National Hockey League's Penguins play their first game, losing 2-1 to the Montreal Canadiens. Pittsburgh was granted an NHL franchise when the league doubled to 12 teams.

Oct. 15, 1967 The Four Tops

Oct. 24, 1967 The Pittsburgh Pipers play their first American Basketball Association game. The team lasts one season before relocating to Minnesota.

Nov. 18, 1967 Beer sales are allowed for first time. It took an act of the state Legislature to permit the sale of beer in city-owned stadiums and arenas.

Feb. 3, 1968 The Penguins play before their first sellout home crowd.

May 4, 1968 The Pipers win the first ABA championship behind the play of future NBA Hall-of-Famer Connie Hawkins, defeating the New Orleans Buccaneers 122-113.

May 12, 1968 Tony Bennett

Oct. 3, 1968 Aretha Franklin

Oct. 12, 1968 The Igloo Club, a high-end lounge with banquet facilities, opens.

Oct. 28, 1968 Richard M. Nixon, the Republicans' presidential candidate, appears in the final days of his campaign. He loses Pennsylvania but wins the general election a week later.

Nov. 17, 1968 Smokey Robinson & The Miracles

Nov. 29, 1968 Steppenwolf

March 9, 1969 The Temptations

July 26, 1969 CLO presents the final show at arena, *How Now, Dow Jones*. With poor acoustics and no rafters for hanging stage pieces, the arena fails to live up to its expectations. The CLO eventually moves to the renovated Heinz Hall, Downtown.

Aug. 1, 1969 Lawrence Welk performs the first of six shows.

Aug. 22, 1969 Dionne Warwick

Sept. 20, 1969 The Doors

Nov. 2, 1969 Janis Joplin makes her only arena appearance.

Dec. 11, 1969 Crosby, Stills, Nash & Young

Feb. 6, 1970 Three Dog Night

March 30, 1970 Led Zeppelin

April 24, 1970 Engelbert Humperdinck

July 31, 1970 Johnny Mathis

Aug. 14 1970 Chicago, with James Taylor

Oct. 16, 1970 Peter, Paul & Mary

Nov. 28, 1970 Sly & the Family Stone

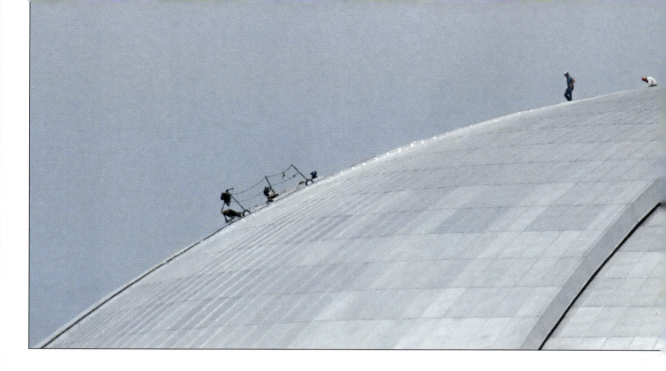

In the early 1980s, then-Penguins owner Edward J. DeBartolo Sr. threatened to move the team and the Spirit, his indoor soccer franchise, but stayed after the city and county reduced his arena rent and agreed to pay for improvements there. DeBartolo, known as the father of the American shopping mall, had purchased the Pens in 1978 and immediately sought to develop the land around the Civic Arena. He negotiated a 50-year lease on the building and won rights to build on its surface parking lots. Those plans never paid off. The Youngstown, Ohio, businessman sold the team in November 1991. JAMES M. KUBUS

JAMES M. KUBUS

PHILIP G. PAVELY

THE ARENA'S MANY MAKEOVERS

1975 Balcony seating, restrooms and concession areas added

1985 Restroom stalls and sinks added; concession stands remodeled; dome cleaned and sealed; concert stage replaced; ice rink refrigeration system installed; parking lots renovated; hockey dashboards replaced

1991 Press box expanded; heating and cooling systems upgraded; ramps added to Levels B and C; steps added to upper parking lot

1993-94 Lighting and sound system improvements; escalator replaced; lots repaved; seating capacity expanded to more than 17,000. The arena was built with 10,500 seats

1997 Club seat and lounge improvements; expansions to concourses and concession stands

JAMES M. KUBUS

ON WITH THE SHOW
CHAPTER FOUR

IN JULY 1962, THE PITTSBURGH CIVIC LIGHT OPERA BEGAN ITS EIGHT-YEAR RESIDENCE IN THE CIVIC ARENA with audiences sitting in 6,629 bright red seats to watch the *Carol Burnett Revue*, a touring show headlined by the popular television star that featured Squirrel Hill native and comedian Marty Allen and his partner Steve Rossi.

But the dream of a permanent home quickly turned into a nightmare.

Opening the dome at intermission always drew applause from theatergoers, but added $200 to the budget — about $1,400 in today's dollars — and hampered performances.

The wind whipped the act curtain and played havoc with the sound system and set pieces.

The soaring, multipurpose hall lacked intimacy, made it difficult for performers to be heard and for audiences to see.

When riots erupted in the Hill District following Martin Luther King Jr.'s assassination in April 1968, audiences became wary of traveling to the Civic Arena.

The 1968 Civic Light Opera season ended with debts totaling a quarter of a million dollars. During 1969, the CLO's final season in the arena consisted of three touring shows — two musicals, plus comedians Dan Rowan & Dick Martin & the *Sock It To Me Gang* from the television show *Laugh-In*.

After a two-year hiatus, Civic Light Opera returned in 1972 with a full, seven-production season in a new, more artistically accommodating location — the former Loew's Penn Theater, renovated and reopened as Heinz Hall.

CLO ARCHIVES · HEINZ HISTORY CENTER ARCHIVES

April 12, 1971 The Grateful Dead performs the first of nine appearances at the arena.

April 29, 1971 Johnny Cash and wife June Carter set an attendance record for a country music show at the arena, attracting 13,076 fans.

July 12, 1971 *Jesus Christ Superstar* opens. The show started out as a best-selling album, and the Pittsburgh performance led to a full-blown Broadway production that opened October 12, 1971.

July 30, 1971 The Jackson 5 performs the first of many concerts by the Jackson family members. Michael Jackson played three consecutive performances in 1988.

July 31, 1971 Glen Campbell

Aug. 10, 1971 The Who

Aug. 14, 1971 Osmond Brothers

Sept. 18, 1971 Black Sabbath

Oct. 8, 1971 Neil Diamond performs at the arena, for the first of a record-setting 18 performances.

Dec. 27, 1971 Alice Cooper

Jan. 28, 1972 Traffic

April 19, 1972 The Carpenters

July 21, 1972 National Wrestling Federation holds first event at the arena, featuring Manuel Soto, Frank Durso, Chief White Owl & Tony Altomare.

Aug. 15, 1972 Sonny & Cher

Aug. 25, 1972 Deep Purple

Sept. 16, 1972 Conway Twitty and Loretta Lynn

Nov. 7, 1972 Yes

June 19, 1973 The dome is opened for Pink Floyd's *Dark Side of the Moon*, giving fans a glimpse of the real moon.

June 25, 1973 Elvis Presley performs first of two consecutive shows. A plaque, paid for by his fans and later hung in the arena, says, "A legendary performer who earned the love and respect of millions. His presence will always be missed."

Sept. 22, 1973 Liza Minnelli

Nov. 28, 1973 A Soviet Youth Exhibition opens, part of dual traveling exhibits in the United States and Soviet Union to help the Cold War enemies understand each other better. The exhibit stays through Christmas.

When the arena first opened, it featured a retractable stage hidden beneath seats, which marveled visitors. For concerts, the seats could be raised 30 feet in the air by hydraulic lifts at either side of the floor. The stage was not very popular for shows, mainly because it sat along the long side of the arena, rather than at one of the ends where performers typically set up. The area beneath the seats was converted into the West Lounge during the 1990s, creating a bar and lounge area for fans who sit in the club level seats.

CARNEGIE MELLON UNIVERSITY ARCHITECTURE ARCHIVES

REMEMBERING THE ARENA

In 1968 **Lenora Nemetz** earned her Equity card while working as a member of the Pittsburgh Civic Light Opera ensemble. The Sheraden native appeared in three shows that season: *My Fair Lady, The Pajama Game* and *Sweet Charity*. A singer, dancer and actress, she has worked on Broadway and in more than two dozen CLO shoes.

"It was an enormous venue, and it was very exciting because it was my first professional job, and I was working with a lot of stars," says Nemetz. "What I loved about the arena — once you got up the hill — was that it was for the whole day. We used to pull seats up in the auditorium and take a nap."

Stage, film and television actress **Sandy Duncan** played Jean MacLaren in the 1965 CLO production of *Brigadoon* at the Civic Arena. What she remembers best about her appearance isn't the role.

"The only memory I have is trying to keep the damn wedding veil thing from falling off my head," she says.

More vivid is "...the amazing opening of that dome. I had just come from doing Zaneeta in *The Music Man* at St. Louis Light Opera, so I just assumed all theaters outside of Texas (where I had worked professionally for five years) must be done under the stars with bugs and rain and everything else that comes with no roof."

When Pittsburgh Civic Light Opera made its Civic Arena debut with the touring production of *The Carol Burnett Revue*, comedian **Marty Allen** and his then partner **Steve Rossi** were part of the show.

"Oh, yeah, that was a great show," says Rossi, a former Squirrel Hill resident who now lives in Las Vegas. "I did a number with her that stopped the show every night. Her husband, the producer said, 'Maybe you should team up with her.'"

During the 1968 Civic Light Opera season at the Civic Arena, Broadway actress **Chita Rivera** played the title role in *Sweet Charity*.

"I keep telling kids that it's a pity that they missed that time — all the tents and civic arenas. The Civic Arena was one of the first times I worked in that situation. It taught me lessons in how to communicate," Rivera says. "All those kids who worked backstage, what a wonderful experience for them."

Civic Light Opera performances at the arena

1962
Carol Burnett Revue *July 2-7*
Jerry Lewis Revue *July 10-15*
Flower Drum Song *July 17-22*
Can-Can *July 24-29*
Fanny *July 31-August 5*
Gypsy *August 7-12*
Oklahoma! *August 14-19*
Song of Norway *August 21-26*
Harry Belafonte *August 27-September 2*

1963
Robert Goulet Revue *July 8-14*
The Firefly *July 16-21*
Carousel *July 23-28*
The Music Man *July 30-August 4*
The Merry Widow *August 6-11*
Wonderful Town *August 13-18*
The Unsinkable Molly Brown *August 20-25*
Nat "King" Cole Revue *August 27-September 1*

1964
Nat "King" Cole Revue *July 6-11*
The Sound of Music *July 13-18*
Top Banana *July 20-25*
Mr. President *July 27-August 1*
My Fair Lady *August 3-8*
Tovarich *August 10-15*
South Pacific *August 17-22*
Arthur Godfrey Revue *August 24-29*

1965
Oliver! *June 28- July 3*
Camelot *July 5-10*
Porgy and Bess *July 12-17*
Little Me *July 19-24*
Brigadoon *July 26-31*
The King and I *August 2-7*
The Student Prince *August 9-14*
West Side Story *August 16-21*
Kismet *August 23-28*

Though built to host just about any type event, the Civic Arena was not ideally suited to any one of them. It never really worked as a venue for musical theater. Audiences complained they couldn't see or hear well. Intimate concerts were impossible. Orchestral performances only accentuated the dome's poor acoustics. Hockey practices were disrupted by the multitude of events, and uneven lighting because of the shape of the dome drove goalies crazy.

DRS ARCHITECTS INCORPORATED (FORMERLY MITCHELL & RITCHEY)

1966
The Great Waltz *July 4-9*
Oklahoma! *July 11-16*
The Desert Song *July 18-23*
The Most Happy Fella *July 25-30*
How to Succeed in Business Without Really Trying *August 1-6*
Robert Goulet Revue *August 8-13*
Guys and Dolls *August 15-20*
Show Boat *August 22-27*

1967
Jack Benny Show *July 10-15*
West Side Story *July 17-22*
Wayne Newton Show *July 24-29*
On a Clear Day You Can See Forever *July 31-August 5*
Song of Norway *August 7-12*
Funny Girl *August 14-19*
Bye Bye Birdie *August 21-26*
Liberace *August 28-September 2*

1968
Jane Morgan Show *July 8-13*
Sound of Music *July 15-20*
The Pajama Game *July 22-27*
Kiss Me, Kate *July 29-August 3*
The New Moon *August 5-10*
My Fair Lady *August 12-17*
Sweet Charity *August 19-24*
Sid Caesar & Imogene Coca Show *August 26-31*

1969
The Happy Time *July 7-12*
Rowan & Martin & the "Sock It To Me Gang" *July 16-19*
How Now, Dow Jones *July 21-26*

1970
(Dark)

1971
(Dark)

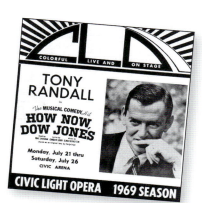

The Hornets returned to Pittsburgh in 1961, the average attendance that season was 4,877 despite the arena's capacity at the time of 10,732. Spectators were treated to sloppy hockey — the Hornets won only six times at home. BOB RATHKE

ICEMEN
CHAPTER FIVE

THEATER MAGNATE JOHN HARRIS BROUGHT PROFESSIONAL HOCKEY BACK TO PITTSBURGH AND IN THE PROCESS, PUT GLAMOUR ON THE ICE.

Born into a family that owned a lucrative chain of theaters, Harris revitalized Duquesne Gardens, Pittsburgh's primary sports and entertainment venue, when he took over management in 1932. He bought a minor-league hockey team, the Detroit Olympics, in 1936, moved it to Pittsburgh and renamed it the Hornets.

Because hockey was only mildly popular, Harris bolstered ticket sales when he paid Olympic figure skating champion Sonja Henie $2,000 to perform during intermissions. She quickly sold out hockey games, leading Harris to form the Ice Capades, a lavish skating show, in 1940.

The Hornets won two American Hockey League championships under Harris, but the team disbanded in 1956 when the dilapidated Duquesne Gardens was torn down.

JOHN HARRIS

Harris was instrumental in making sure the new arena would have a hockey-friendly design, and his Hornets resumed play in the building weeks after it opened in 1961.

"I can assure you of one thing — that the expenditure of money will be no deterrent in relation to getting the best," Harris vowed at the time. "Pittsburgh is the best city with the best arena, so it must have the best hockey club."

The revived Hornets' first season was awful, setting AHL records for futility: Most times shut out in a season (9); most games lost in a season (58); and most games lost at home (27). The Hornets finished in last place with the fewest wins in team history (10).

During its second season, the team doubled its wins but still finished last in the Western Division.

Frustrated, Harris sold the team to the Detroit Red Wings in April 1963. The Hornets remained in Pittsburgh as Detroit's farm club.

Vic Stasiuk (20) was a player for the Hornets and also the head coach, leading the team to a 40-29-3 record in 1963-64 to finish first in the Western Division. Warren Godfrey (3) was a rugged defenseman who played in 57 games. BOB RATHKE

The NHL awarded a franchise to Pittsburgh on February 8, 1966. The Hornets played a final game in the arena on April 30, 1967, when the team won the league championship on a goal scored by Billy Harris 26 seconds into overtime — the final goal in the 26-season history of the franchise.

John Harris lived above the arena at Washington Plaza Apartments until his death on February 12, 1969, at age 70.

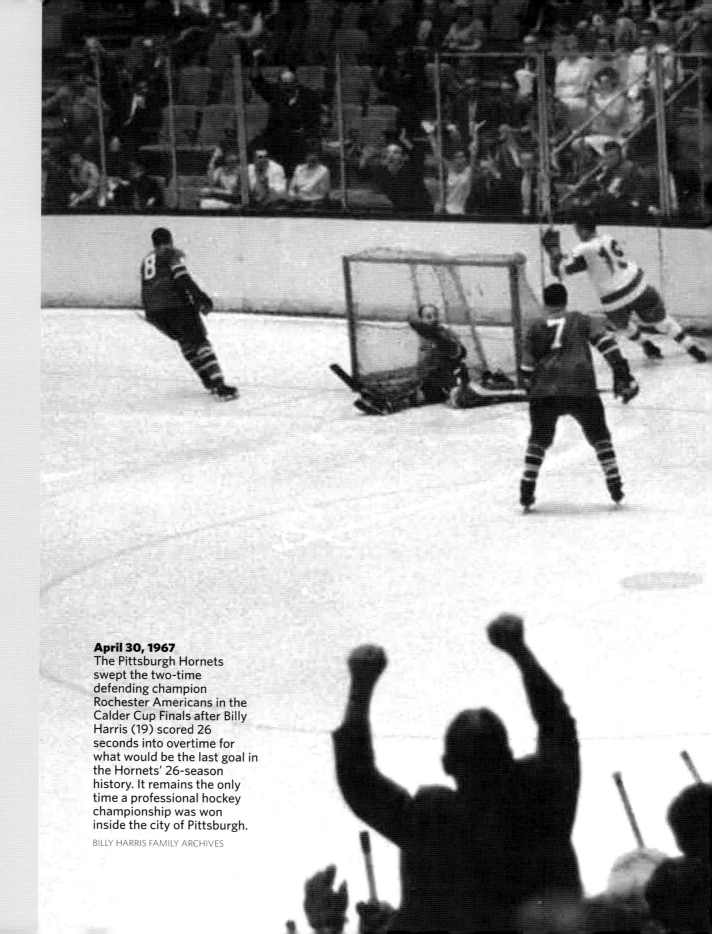

May 7, 1974 The Pittsburgh Triangles World Team Tennis debuts. Although the professional tennis league is founded by Pittsburghers, the franchise lasts just three seasons.

June 23, 1974 The Byzantine Catholic Diocese of Pittsburgh celebrates its 50th anniversary at the arena.

July 13, 1974 Gladys Knight & The Pips

Aug. 20, 1974 Rush

Oct. 3, 1974 Kool and the Gang

Oct. 25, 1974 ZZ Top

Nov. 12, 1974 Elton John performs the first of six shows at the arena, through 2006.

Nov. 19, 1974 David Bowie

June 13, 1975 The Penguins declare bankruptcy for the first time. Speculation builds that the team will relocate, perhaps to Seattle.

June 28, 1975 The Bee Gees

June 30, 1975 Eric Clapton and Santana

July 11, 1975 New owners — Al Savill, Otto Frenzel & Wren Blair — bring the Penguins out of bankruptcy.

Sept. 25, 1975 The arena capacity is boosted by 3,000 with the addition of the E-level balconies.

Feb. 14, 1976 Joni Mitchell

April 17, 1976 Lynyrd Skynyrd

Sept. 4, 1976 Kiss

Nov. 10, 1976 Aerosmith

Dec. 31, 1976 Elvis Presley plays a New Year's Eve concert. Fans remember this as one of the best performances from the latter part of Elvis' career. He died eight months later on August 16.

Feb. 17, 1977 Electric Light Orchestra

March 10, 1977 Genesis

July 27, 1977 Eagles

March 23, 1978 John Denver

April 5, 1978 Edward J. DeBartolo Sr. takes ownership of the Penguins. DeBartolo keeps the team through its first Stanley Cup championship in 1991.

June 15, 1978 Foreigner

Aug. 10, 1978 Boston

Dec. 11, 1978 Billy Joel

Dec. 14, 1978 Styx

Jan. 23, 1979 Penguins negotiate a nine-year arena lease.

April 30, 1967
The Pittsburgh Hornets swept the two-time defending champion Rochester Americans in the Calder Cup Finals after Billy Harris (19) scored 26 seconds into overtime for what would be the last goal in the Hornets' 26-season history. It remains the only time a professional hockey championship was won inside the city of Pittsburgh.

BILLY HARRIS FAMILY ARCHIVES

Hornets Records: 1961-67 ■ CHAMPIONSHIP SEASON

season	COMPLETE SEASON					AT THE ARENA				
	REGULAR SEASON			PLAYOFFS		REGULAR SEASON			PLAYOFFS	
	W	L	T	W	L	W	L	T	W	L
1961-62	10	58	2	—	—	6	27	2	—	—
1962-63	20	48	4	—	—	16	17	3	—	—
1963-64	40	29	3	1	4	26	8	2	1	1
1964-65	29	36	7	1	3	18	14	4	1	1
1965-66	38	31	1	0	3	21	14	1	0	1
1966-67	38	33	1	8	1	24	8	4	5	0

The Hornets' three Calder Cup championships are noted on a banner that was hung from the dome on February 3, 2001. The banner stayed up for two years and then was stored on the floor of the gondola near the roof.

JAMES M. KUBUS

Pittsburgh Penguins alumni players and the 2009-10 team gather at center ice before the regular season finale April 8, 2010. CHAZ PALLA

THE PENGUINS

Of all the athletes and performers to grace the arena, none of them embodied the building like the Pittsburgh Penguins.

The Penguins weren't just the arena's primary tenant — they got their name from its distinctive igloo design.

Coincidentally, the Pens lost their first and last arena games to the very same team: the Montreal Canadiens, 2-1, on October 11, 1967, and again to the Canadiens, 5-2, on May 12, 2010.

None of the Pens' Stanley Cup crowns in 1991, 1992 and 2009 was clinched at the arena, but the building, fondly dubbed the Igloo, witnessed some of hockey's greatest moments.

The 1990 National Hockey League All-Star game — the only mid-season classic played at the arena — saw Mario Lemieux score four goals to power the Wales Conference to a 12-7 win over the Wayne Gretzky-led Campbell Conference all-stars. It was the first time a national audience saw Lemieux and Gretzky in the same game.

Andy Bathgate scored the first goal in Penguins franchise history against the Montreal Canadiens on October 11, 1967. BOB RATHKE

McGREGOR

The arena hosted the 1997 National Hockey League Draft. It also witnessed the third-longest game in NHL history, when the Lemieux-less Pens lost in five overtimes to the Flyers, 2-1, on May 4, 2000, in the Eastern Conference semifinals.

Pro hockey came to Pittsburgh, thanks to state Senator Jack E. McGregor and friend Peter Block, who lobbied for a franchise during the NHL's six-team expansion for the 1967-68 season.

It came down to two cities for the final bid.

The Steel City got the nod over Buffalo, bringing the NHL back for the first time since the Pittsburgh Pirates hockey team departed in 1930.

The team's name was picked from a 26,000-entry, name-the-team contest.

McGregor's wife, Carol, thought Penguins was fitting because the Civic Arena was nicknamed the Igloo because of its stainless steel dome.

The Eskimos drew some support. "Eskimos live in an Igloo," said Jack Riley, the club's first general manager. But McGregor and the wives of some of the team's owners settled on the Penguins.

"I didn't think too much of it at the time," said Riley. "I was busy putting the team together. But a lot of people didn't like it. Our coach, Red Sullivan, really didn't like it."

Eventually, people warmed to the name and to the team's logo of a Penguin skating on a golden triangle.

Peter Schepis parades Penguin Pete, an Ecuadorian-born penguin on loan from the Pittsburgh Aquazoo, during intermission in October 1971. The Penguins were one of the first professional sports teams to have a live mascot. PITTSBURGHHOCKEY.NET

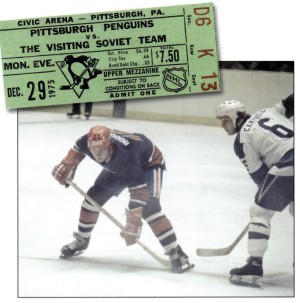

The Soviet Wings Aleksandr Budunov and the Penguins Colin Campbell during an international event, USSR vs. NHL on December 29, 1975. The Wings won, 7-4, in front of 13,210 fans.
PITTSBURGHHOCKEY.NET

Fans lean over the glass to get involved as the Penguins battle the St. Louis Blues during the season finale April 2, 1972. The Pens won the game, 6-2, and helped secure the final playoff spot in the West Division. PITTSBURGHHOCKEY.NET

April 19, 1979 The Village People kick off their U.S. tour at the arena.

Aug. 17, 1979 Kansas performs the first of two back-to-back concerts.

Nov. 26, 1979 Fleetwood Mac

Dec. 7, 1979 The Pittsburgh Spirit play the first Major Indoor Soccer League game at the arena.

May 10, 1980 Journey performs for the first time with the British rock band The Babys.

July 14, 1980 Heart

Sept. 21, 1980 The arena receives new scoreboard.

Nov. 30, 1980 Bruce Springsteen & E Street Band perform the first of two consecutive concerts.

Nov. 9, 1980 Stevie Wonder performs the first of his two arena shows.

Feb. 16, 1981 Cheap Trick with UFO

April 18, 1981 REO Speedwagon

May 15, 1981 Penguins owner Ed DeBartolo Sr. negotiates a 50-year arena lease, with rights to develop the surface parking lots outside. He takes over management of the arena two months later.

July 5, 1981 The arena dome is cleaned.

July 14, 1981 Van Halen

Aug. 4, 1981 Tom Petty & The Heartbreakers

Nov. 6, 1981 Boxer Larry Holmes wins a TKO against Renaldo Snipes.

Jan. 13, 1982 *Sesame Street Live* opens eight shows over five days, becoming an annual attraction.

Feb. 2, 1982 Ozzy Osbourne

April 9, 1982 The Police

Oct. 21, 1982 Diana Ross performs the first of two shows.

Feb. 1, 1983 U.S. Figure Skating championships, known as *The Great Skate* are held at the arena. Scott Hamilton wins the men's gold, while Rosalynn Sumners wins the women's gold.

Feb. 28, 1983 Prince

March 5, 1983 Hall & Oates

June 12, 1983 Southern Baptist Convention meets.

Sept. 17, 1983 Lionel Richie

Nov. 30, 1983 AC/DC

Feb. 28, 1984 Duran Duran

Oct. 17, 1984 Penguins Mario Lemieux plays his first game at the arena, after being drafted first overall in June.

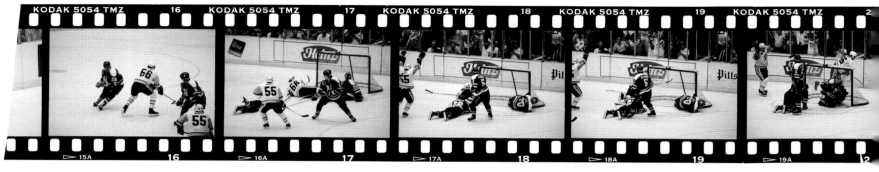

Mario Lemieux scored the signature goal of his career during Game 2 of the 1991 Stanley Cup Final against the Minnesota North Stars on May 17, 1991. Lemieux carried the puck through the neutral zone, split two Minnesota defenders and slipped the puck past twisted goalie Jon Casey. The goal gave the Penguins a 3-1 lead en route to a 4-1 victory that tied the series and propelled the Pens to their first Stanley Cup Championship.   JAMES M. KUBUS

Lemieux registered a team-high in scoring during the 1988-89 season with 199 points (85 goals and 114 assists) en route to his second consecutive Art Ross Trophy for leading scorer.

JAMES M. KUBUS

Austin Lemieux watches as his father's retirement banner is lowered from the arena rafters December 27, 2000. The Hall-of-Famer returned to play after a three-year hiatus.
CHRISTOPHER HORNER

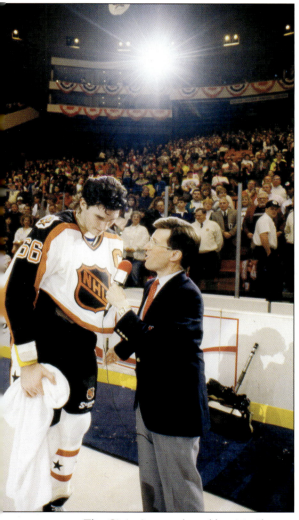

The Civic Arena played host to the NHL All-Star Game for the first time on January 21, 1990. Lemieux scored four goals on his way to his third All-Star MVP Award. JAMES M. KUBUS

SUPER MARIO

Mario Lemieux, the No. 1 overall draft pick in 1984, played 17 seasons at the Igloo, and he stole the show night after night. His achievements are some of the greatest in club history.

He notched three five-goal games at the arena. He scored five different ways on New Year's Eve 1988 against the New Jersey Devils. He netted five goals in a 10-7 victory over the Flyers in the 1989 playoffs and in an 8-4 win over the St. Louis Blues on March 26, 1996. He had two six-assist games and recorded 21 of his 40 career hat tricks in the Igloo.

There also was his four-goal effort in the NHL All-Star game in 1990, two Stanley Cup title runs in 1990-91 and 1991-92, and his 600th career goal, which came against Vancouver, on February 4, 1997.

Lemieux brought the Penguins out of bankruptcy in 1999. In arguably the most memorable regular-season moment, Lemieux returned from a 44-month retirement on December 27, 2000, to a deafening crowd. In his first 33 seconds on the ice, he set up a goal against the Maple Leafs.

Oct. 28, 1984 Alabama with Juice Newton

April 9, 1985 U2

May 28, 1985 Madonna

July 19, 1985 Air Supply

Aug. 23, 1985 Tina Turner

Oct. 2, 1985 Ratt and Bon Jovi perform. Bon Jovi played at the arena 13 times.

Nov. 28, 1985 The city and county borrow $12 million for arena renovations.

Nov. 28, 1985 John Cougar Mellencamp

June 24, 1986 Jimmy Buffet & the Coral Reefer Band

June 28, 1986 After a concert by Run DMC, 25 people are arrested and 22 treated at hospitals after fans rampage through Downtown.

July 8, 1986 Windham Hill

Aug. 22, 1986 The Jimmy Swaggart Evangelistic Crusade is broadcast from the arena. Swaggart's hour-long prayer services made him the nation's most popular television preacher at the time.

Sept. 25, 1986 David Lee Roth with Cinderella

Jan. 9, 1987 A parents' room opens for concerts, giving moms and dads a place to stay while their children attend the Iron Maiden concert.

March 26, 1987 Pittsburgh Art Commission seeks historic designation for the arena.

April 23, 1987 *Muppet Babies Live* opens at arena for the first time, becoming an annual attraction.

June 19, 1987 The Pittsburgh Gladiators play their first Arena Football League game. The Gladiators were one of four original teams in the new league.

July 30, 1987 Whitney Houston with Kenny G

July 31, 1987 Motley Crüe with Whitesnake

Aug. 1, 1987 The arena hosts ArenaBowl I, the AFL championship. The Gladiators lose to the Denver Dynamite, 45-16.

Oct. 23, 1987 R.E.M. with 10,000 Maniacs

Nov. 5, 1987 Aerosmith with Dokken

March 26, 1988 Frank Sinatra and Sammy Davis Jr.

The Penguins gather at center ice with the Stanley Cup to hoist the team's second set of championship banners.
JAMES M. KUBUS

The ice preparation takes more than 10 hours to complete. Starting with a thin layer of water followed with a layer of white paint, colored lines and logos are all painted by hand. When finished the ice surface is about three-quarters of an inch thick.
KEITH HODAN

Ron Francis, left, is congratulated by Jaromir Jagr after Francis set up a goal by Fredrik Olausson on March 21, 1998. Francis became the seventh player in NHL history to record his 1,000th assist. The Pens defeated the Flyers, 4-3, to become the 10th team with 1,000 wins. JAMES M. KUBUS

Pens goaltender Tom Barrasso and defenseman Paul Coffey were an integral tandem in the team's first championship in 1991. Barrasso holds the franchise record for most games played in goal (726), the most wins (226), and the most shutouts (22). Coffey's 113 points in 1988 set the team record for scoring in a season by a defenseman (30 goals + 83 assists). Coffey was inducted into the Hockey Hall of Fame in 2004. JAMES M. KUBUS

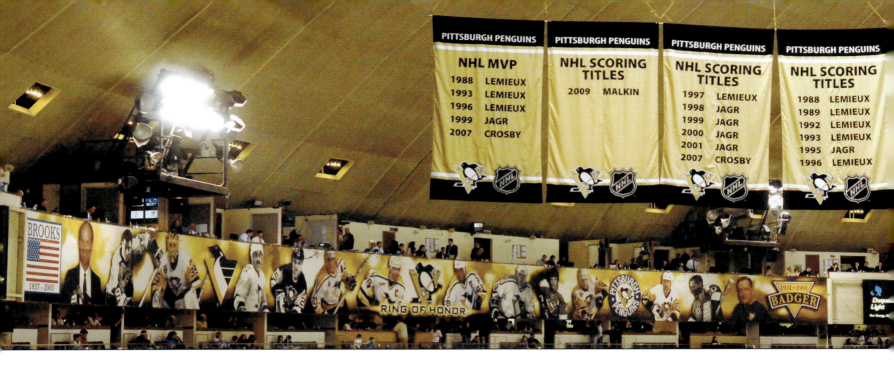

All-time Penguins' legends were recognized on the Ring Of Honor below press row while 13 scoring titles and five league MVP awards hung from the ceiling.

In a view from the crow's nest, high above the scoreboard, the Pens go through a morning skate during the playoffs in their last season.

JAMES M. KUBUS

Hall of Fame announcer Mike Lange delivers his broadcast from above the ice. Lange has called Pens games since 1974. JAMES M. KUBUS

A trail of hydraulic fluid from a malfunctioning Zamboni caused a half-hour delay to the start of a game on February 24, 2008. CHAZ PALLA

Penguins equipment manager Dana Heinze prepares the dressing room before a 2010 playoff game. JAMES M. KUBUS

JOHN BARBERO

From his drawn-out pronunciation of Mario Lemieux's last name to his unforgettable calls of Sidney Crosby's goals, John Barbero was synonymous with Penguins hockey since 1972. The former high school principal worked more than 800 games in the Igloo as the Penguins' public address announcer. Barbero of Roscoe, Washington County, gave up the job during the 2009-10 season because he was battling an inoperable brain tumor. Barbero died July 26, 2010. He was 64.

In his arena debut Sidney Crosby scores his first NHL goal October 8, 2005, against Hannu Toivonen of the Boston Bruins. CHAZ PALLA

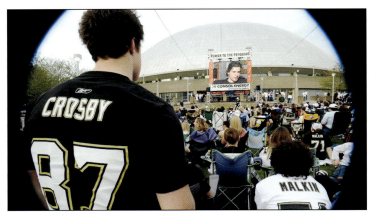

Penguins fans gather outside the arena to watch a playoff game on the outdoor TV against the New York Rangers April 25, 2008. The Penguins won 5-4 and went on to win the series 4-1.
CHRISTOPHER HORNER

SID THE KID

Once arriving in Pittsburgh in 2005 as one of the most highly anticipated draft picks in NHL history, Sidney Crosby became the Igloo's next superstar.

The No. 1 overall pick was named the league's Most Valuable Player in his second season, 2006-07.

Crosby brought the Penguins one step closer to the 2009 Stanley Cup when he scored the game-winning goal at home in a 4-2 Game 4 victory over the Red Wings on June, 4, 2009.

Crosby played 185 games at the arena, totaling 101 goals and 182 assists. He posted a career-high five assists in an 8-4 victory over the Flyers on December 13, 2006, and recorded three hat tricks at the arena during the 2009-10 season in wins over the Sabres, the Rangers and the Canadiens.

"Throughout Christmastime, all the stockings on the ice and hearing Christmas music. That was the first I ever heard Christmas music after a goal."

— *Sidney Crosby, forward, recalls his favorite moment at the arena.*

Penguins Records: 1967-2010

■ CHAMPIONSHIP SEASON

COMPLETE SEASON | AT THE ARENA

	REGULAR SEASON					PLAYOFFS		REGULAR SEASON					PLAYOFFS	
season	W	L	T	OTL	OT	W	L	W	L	T	RT	OT	W	L
1967-68	27	34	13	—	—	—	—	15	12	10	—	—	—	—
1968-69	20	45	11	—	—	—	—	12	20	6	—	—	—	—
1969-70	26	38	12	—	—	6	4	17	13	8	—	—	4	1
1970-71	21	37	20	—	—	—	—	18	12	9	—	—	—	—
1971-72	26	38	14	—	—	0	4	18	15	6	—	—	2	2
1972-73	32	37	9	—	—	—	—	24	11	4	—	—	—	—
1973-74	28	41	9	—	—	—	—	15	18	6	—	—	—	—
1974-75	37	28	15	—	—	5	4	25	5	10	—	—	3	2
1975-76	35	33	12	—	—	1	2	23	11	6	—	—	1	0
1976-77	34	33	13	—	—	1	2	22	12	6	—	—	0	2
1977-78	25	37	18	—	—	—	—	16	15	9	—	—	—	—
1978-79	36	31	13	—	—	2	5	23	12	5	—	—	0	3
1979-80	30	37	13	—	—	2	3	20	13	7	—	—	1	1
1980-81	30	37	13	—	—	2	3	21	16	3	—	—	1	1
1981-82	31	36	13	—	—	2	3	21	11	8	—	—	2	0
1982-83	18	53	9	—	—	—	—	14	22	4	—	—	—	—
1983-84	16	58	6	—	—	—	—	7	29	4	—	—	—	—
1984-85	24	51	5	—	—	—	—	17	20	3	—	—	—	—
1985-86	34	38	8	—	—	—	—	20	15	5	—	—	—	—
1986-87	30	38	12	—	—	—	—	19	15	6	—	—	—	—
1987-88	36	35	9	—	—	—	—	22	12	6	—	—	—	—
1988-89	40	33	7	—	—	7	4	24	13	3	—	—	4	2
1989-90	32	40	8	—	—	—	—	22	15	3	—	—	—	—
1990-91	41	33	6	—	—	16	8	25	12	3	—	—	9	4
1991-92	39	32	9	—	—	16	5	21	13	6	—	—	8	2
1992-93	56	21	7	—	—	7	5	31	6	4	—	—	5	2
1993-94	44	27	13	—	—	2	4	24	9	8	—	—	2	1
1994-95*	29	16	3	—	—	5	7	18	5	1	—	—	4	3
1995-96	49	29	4	—	—	11	7	32	9	0	—	—	5	5
1996-97	38	36	8	—	—	1	4	25	11	5	—	—	1	1
1997-98	40	24	18	—	—	2	4	21	10	10	—	—	1	2
1998-99	38	30	14	—	—	6	7	21	10	10	—	—	3	3
1999-00	37	37	8	6	—	6	5	23	11	7	0	—	2	3
2000-01	42	28	9	3	—	9	9	24	15	2	0	—	—	—
2001-02	28	41	8	5	—	—	—	16	20	4	1	—	—	—
2002-03	27	44	6	5	—	—	—	15	22	2	2	—	—	—
2003-04	23	47	8	4	—	—	—	13	22	6	0	—	—	—
2004-05**														
2005-06	22	46	—	—	14	—	—	12	21	—	—	8	—	—
2006-07	47	24	—	—	11	1	4	26	10	—	—	5	0	2
2007-08	47	27	—	—	8	14	6	26	9	—	—	5	9	2
2008-09	45	28	—	—	9	16	8	25	13	—	—	3	9	2
2009-10	47	27	—	—	10	7	6	25	12	—	—	4	3	4

TOTALS

* strike-shortened season
** a labor dispute forced the cancellation of the entire season

April 10, 1988 City Council considers a name change to the Richard S. Caliguiri Arena after the mayor is diagnosed with the protein disorder amyloidosis. Caliguiri dies on May 6.

July 17, 1988 David Lee Roth with Poison

Aug. 7, 1988 INXS

Sept. 26, 1988 Michael Jackson opens three concerts at the arena, drawing more than 50,000 fans.

Dec. 31, 1988 Lemieux scores five goals, five ways — even-strength, power-play, shorthanded, penalty shot and empty-net.

Feb. 10, 1989 Poison performs with Tesla. This is the second of only two arena appearances for Butler native Bret Michaels.

April 22, 1989 The Detroit Turbos and the New England Blazers play the first Major Indoor Lacrosse League game at the arena.

Dec. 3, 1989 New Kids on the Block with Dino & Cover Girls

Jan. 5, 1990 The Pittsburgh Bulls play their first Major Indoor Lacrosse League game. The franchise lasts four seasons.

Jan. 19, 1990 *Stars on Ice* comes to the arena for the first time, becoming an annual attraction.

Jan. 21, 1990 The 41st NHL All-Star game takes place. Lemieux is named the game MVP for the third time.

Feb. 4, 1990 Paul McCartney returns to the arena for the first time as a solo act, playing Beatles and Wings music for two sold-out concerts.

March 13, 1990 Janet Jackson with Chuckii Booker

July 26, 1990 MC Hammer

Sept. 15, 1990 Luciano Pavarotti plays a benefit concert for the Pittsburgh Opera after he fell ill during a concert months earlier and had to cancel a string of shows.

May 15, 1991 The Penguins play in their first Stanley Cup Final game at the arena, losing 5-4 to the Minnesota North Stars. The Penguins win the series in the sixth game, on the road. It is the team's first championship.

Sept. 28, 1991 *American Gladiators* pits amateur challengers against the show's regular athletes.

Nov. 7, 1991 Paula Abdul

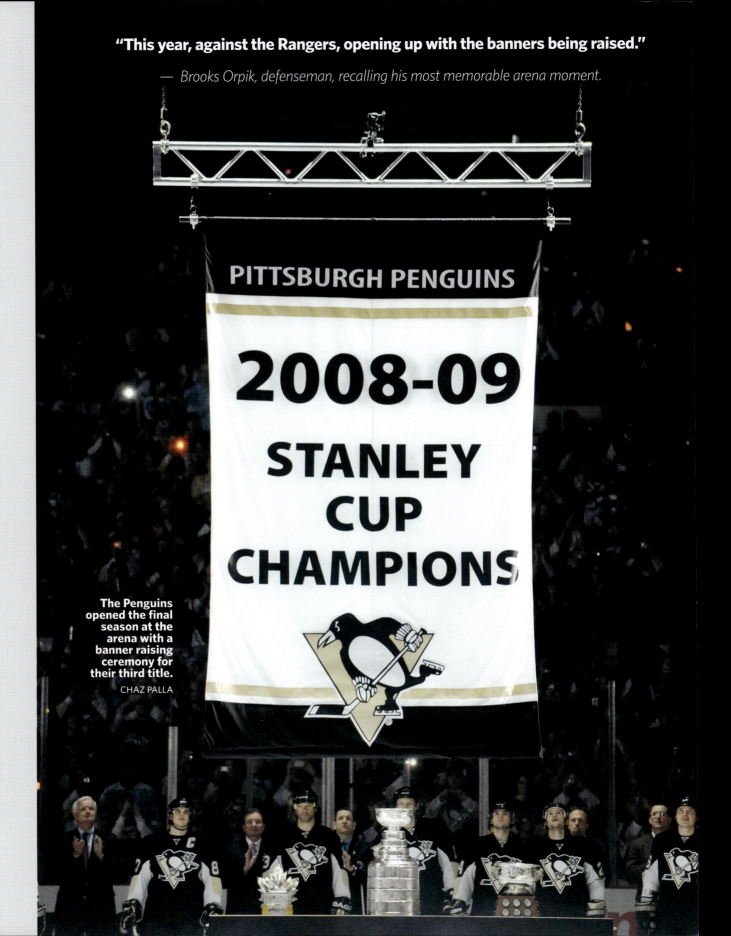

"This year, against the Rangers, opening up with the banners being raised."

— *Brooks Orpik, defenseman, recalling his most memorable arena moment.*

The Penguins opened the final season at the arena with a banner raising ceremony for their third title.

CHAZ PALLA

Goalie Marc-Andre Fleury made an incredible 46 saves — including a penalty shot, in his October 10, 2003, NHL and arena debut as the youngest goalie in the league — despite the 3-0 loss to the Los Angeles Kings. CHAZ PALLA

Evgeni Malkin celebrates his hat trick in the third period in Game 2 of the Eastern Conference final May 21, 2009, against the Carolina Hurricanes. CHAZ PALLA

"When this building kind of gets a roar going, it's pretty fun,"

— *Jordan Staal, forward.*

Jordan Staal deflects a shot past Montreal goaltender Jaroslav Halak to score Pittsburgh's final goal at the arena. JAMES M. KUBUS

FOND FAREWELL

The final numbers for the Penguins games at the arena from 1967-2010.

1,667
Games played

858
Wins

576
Losses

205
Ties

28
Overtime losses/shootout losses

6,133
Goals for

5,369
Goals against

135
Post-season games

80
Post-season wins

55
Post-season losses

May 12, 2010 The final 10th of a second runs off the clock to end a run of hockey that started 48 years, six months and 29 days before when the Pittsburgh Hornets first skated at the arena on October 14, 1961.

JAMES M. KUBUS

Fans of the Pittsburgh Triangles were often treated to an open-air match when the roof opened to reveal the city's skyline.
GEORGE D. HETRICK · PA ROOM CARNEGIE LIBRARY

WHAT A SPORT
CHAPTER SIX

WHEN IT CAME TO SPORTING EVENTS, THE ARENA WASN'T ONLY ABOUT GUYS ON SKATES.

Although the Penguins were the primary tenant, the arena was home to a heavyweight title bout, an American Basketball Association championship, a World Team Tennis crown, two of the first three Arena Football League's ArenaBowls and 12 professional franchises.

The arena hosted the first national all-star high school basketball game, the Roundball Classic, on March 26, 1965, and the 1983 U.S. Figure Skating championships.

Pro wrestlers Bruno Sammartino, Bob Backlund, Hulk Hogan and Kurt Angle plied their craft in front of packed houses. Muhammad Ali, Sugar Ray Robinson and Larry Holmes fought there.

More than 20 National Basketball Association games, including a half-dozen, neutral-site games by the Wilt Chamberlin-led Philadelphia 76ers in 1967, were played at the arena.

The Spirit men's soccer team played from 1978-86, the longest stay by any pro team other than the Penguins.

The Pittsburgh Gladiators, one of four original teams in the AFL, averaged nearly 13,000 fans in four home games of their debut season in 1987.

The Pittsburgh Pipers won the 1968 ABA championship with a 122-113 victory over New Orleans in Game 7 at the arena. The Pipers eventually became the Condors. Although the team folded after the 1971-72 season, its colors lived on. Team jerseys were donated to Attica Prison in Upstate New York for use by inmates.

Nov. 19, 1991 Howard Baldwin takes over ownership of the Penguins. He purchased the team early in its second championship season and was part of the ownership group that declared bankruptcy in 1998.

May 26, 1992 The Penguins open their second Stanley Cup Final series at home, defeating the Chicago Blackhawks, 5-4. The Penguins sweep the series in four games, winning their second championship on the road.

June 22, 1992 The National Baptist Congress opens.

Nov. 7, 1992 Def Leppard

Dec. 30, 1992 Bobby Brown

Aug. 20, 1993 Reba McEntire and Brooks & Dunn perform for the first of three times over five years.

Sept. 15, 1993 Billy Ray Cyrus

Sept. 19, 1993 The Roman Catholic Diocese of Pittsburgh celebrates its 150th birthday. The two-and-a-half-hour ceremony features two Catholic cardinals and 26 bishops. Magenta streamers are draped over the scoreboard and central altar to create a stained-glass look.

Sept. 25, 1993 The arena capacity is boosted by 1,000 with addition of F-level balconies.

Feb. 25, 1994 Magician David Copperfield performs two shows.

April 16, 1994 Alan Jackson

May 29, 1994 Meatloaf

May 20, 1994 Bryan Adams

Sept. 6, 1994 The Filming of *Sudden Death* begins starring Jean-Claude Van Damme as a Pittsburgh firefighter who saves the vice president during a Penguins playoff game.

Feb. 15, 1995 Boys II Men

March 17, 1995 Amy Grant

March 25, 1995 Robert Plant and Jimmy Page

Nov. 24, 1995 Phish

Jan. 1, 1996 Rusted Root

March 14, 1996 Red Hot Chili Peppers

April 16, 1996 Bush, a British alternative-rock band, performs.

Sept. 9, 1996 The Smashing Pumpkins

Oct. 9, 1996 Penguins owner Howard Baldwin threatens to relocate the Penguins unless the arena is renovated. The Allegheny County Regional Asset District approves a $12.9 million upgrade four months later.

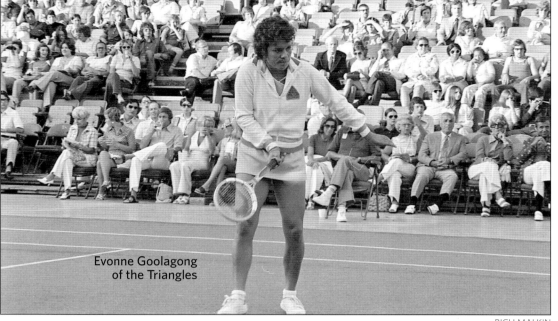

Evonne Goolagong of the Triangles

TENNIS

World Team Tennis brought lots of color to the sport.

Yellow balls replaced the white ones used at every major tournament. Flashy uniforms replaced the starched white ones worn by almost every player. Fans were encouraged to cheer at a time when other venues shushed them.

Even better, said league founder Chuck Reichblum, the Pittsburgh franchise, the Triangles, had a unique venue at the arena when the roof leaves opened during the playing of the National Anthem at the start of most matches.

"It was just amazing how out of thin air all this was created," Reichblum said.

Started in Pittsburgh, the league quickly added teams in New York, Chicago, Los Angeles and a half-dozen other cities.

Teams had creative names, including one that raised a few eyebrows: The arena manager refused to put the Hawaiian Leis' name on the building marquis. Boston took the Lobsters, a word play on the tennis move of hitting the ball high and deep into the opponent's end. The Philadelphia Freedom, coached by Billie Jean King, inspired a song by her friend Elton John. The Triangles lasted just three seasons, from 1974 to 1976.

Billie Jean King

Vitas Gerulaitis of the Triangles

ICE SKATING

Figure skating has a storied history in the arena. The first-ever event there was an Ice Capades show on September 19, 1961.

Many more big nights would follow in glitzy ice shows and in competitive events.

In February 1983, the arena hosted the U.S. Figure Skating Championships. Two-time defending world champion Scott Hamilton held off 19-year-old California sensation Brian Boitano — both future Olympic gold medalists — to win the Senior crown, while 18-year-old Rosalynn Sumners topped defending world champion Elaine Zayak for the women's championship. Winning the gold medal for ice dancing were hometown favorites, Judy Blumberg and Michael Seibert. He was born in Pittsburgh.

In 2004, 19-year-old Evan Lysacek finished fifth in the men's competition at the SmartOnes Skate America competition. He won Olympic gold in 2010.

Russian pairs skater Tatiana Totmianina fell and suffered a concussion after her partner Maxim Marinin lost his balance performing a difficult lift at the SmartOnes Skate America competition October 23, 2004. She didn't remember the accident. They went on to win the 2006 Olympic gold medal in pairs figure skating. AP IMAGES

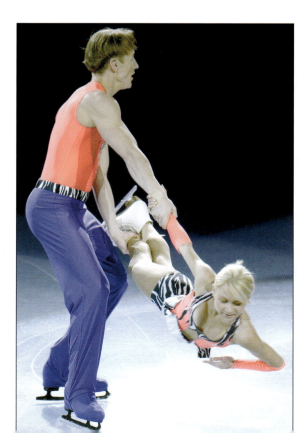

Russian pair Julia Obertas and Sergei Slavnov perform during the free skate Sunday, October 24, 2004, at the SmartOnes Skate America. JASMINE GOLDBAND

Stars on Ice (1997) STEVE KALINSKY

BOXING

The arena didn't have a long history of boxing matches, but it made them count.

Sugar Ray Robinson lost to Joey Archer in a unanimous 10-round decision on November 10, 1965, in the final boxing match of his 202-bout career. It was Robinson's second career bout at the arena. He knocked out Wilf Greaves in the eighth round on December 8, 1961.

Muhammad Ali, then known as Cassius Clay, knocked out Charlie Powell on January 24, 1963. It would be another 13 months before he would beat Sonny Liston — with a packed Civic Arena showing the bout on closed circuit television — to win the heavyweight title and change his name.

In the lone title fight, Larry Holmes knocked out Renaldo Snipes in the 11th round on November 6, 1981, to retain his World Boxing Council heavyweight crown. Snipes had floored Holmes in the seventh round, and, to this day, critics say the 10-count was long.

Many in the arena booed when the fight was stopped in the 11th round.

Cassius Clay knocks out Charlie Powell January 24, 1963.
AP IMAGES

WRESTLING

The Igloo was known for rabid pro wrestling crowds who cheered and booed top stars with gusto.

Studio wrestling in the 1960s was the first to bring wrestlers to the arena. Pittsburgh native Bruno Sammartino was the main attraction, and the World Wide Wrestling Federation supplied the shows. At that time, dozens of other promoters across the country controlled cities or regions.

On June 28, 1998, the arena went into the wrestling history books. A match, *Hell in a Cell*, featuring Mick "Mankind" Foley and Mark "The Undertaker" Calaway took place inside a 16-foot-high cage that surrounded the ring. The Undertaker and Mankind were fighting on the roof of the cage when The Undertaker tossed Mankind. He landed on the Spanish announcer's table 16 feet below, and it shattered. The play-by-play announcer for the English broadcast, Jim Ross, screamed, "Good God, he's gotta be broken in half."

On June 27, 2009, the arena hosted the first Mixed Martial Arts event in Pennsylvania, *Rumble on the Rivers*. With the fighting legalized in the state earlier that year, fight night included an appearance by Tito Ortiz, one of the most popular and accomplished MMA fighters ever.

Mt. Lebanon native Kurt Angle celebrates after beating Steve Austin to win the WWF Championship on September 23, 2001.

"At least once a month the crowd would get so excited and carried away that the police had to haul people out cause they couldn't control themselves."

— John DeFazio, who wrestled as Jumpin Johnny DeFazio during the 1960s and '70s, recalls the arena crowds attending "Studio Wrestling." DeFazio went on to become an official of the United Steelworkers of America and a member of Allegheny County Council.

JOHNNY DEFAZIO ARCHIVES

Nov. 8, 1996 The Who

Jan. 11, 1997 New Edition

March 26, 1997 Metallica

April 4, 1997 Celine Dion

May 4, 1997 Marilyn Manson

June 17, 1997 The NHL draft is held at the arena. The Boston Bruins take center Joe Thornton first overall.

Oct. 1, 1997 Luther Vandross and Vanessa Williams

Oct. 13, 1997 Garth Brooks performs the first of six straight sold-out shows.

Nov. 20, 1997 Allegheny Energy agrees to pay the Penguins $5 million to name the arena the Allegheny Energy Dome. The Public Auditorium Authority owns the building and opposes the deal.

Feb. 8, 1998 The Greek-born composer and musician Yanni performs at the arena.

April 19, 1998 A total of 2,049 young musicians sets the record for world's largest orchestra.

Aug. 27, 1998 Hanson

Oct. 13, 1998 The Penguins file for bankruptcy, again.

Nov. 6, 1998 Tori Amos

Dec. 5, 1998 Vince Gill

Dec. 28, 1998 Barenaked Ladies

Jan. 22, 1999 *Grease on Ice* opens three days of 1950s music and ice dancing at the arena.

Feb. 19, 1999 Black Sabbath

March 8, 1999 *NSYNC

March 14, 1999 Jay-Z with DMX

Sept. 3, 1999 Lemieux forms an ownership group with California billionaire Ron Burkle to bring the Penguins out of bankruptcy.

Dec. 20, 1999 Mellon Financial Corporation agrees to pay $18 million over 10 years for naming rights, changing the Civic Arena name to Mellon Arena.

Jan. 22, 2000 The Pittsburgh CrosseFire plays its first National Lacrosse League game at the arena. The franchise lasts one season.

April 14, 2000 Creed

June 6, 2000 Blink 182

June 27, 2000 Ricky Martin

July 26, 2000 Dr. Dre, Snoop Dogg and Eminem

Sept. 2, 2000 Tim McGraw and Faith Hill

Oct. 15, 2000 Dixie Chicks

Oct. 29, 2000 Stone Temple Pilots

Nov. 28, 2000 Manheim Steamroller bring its holiday music show to the arena during the week after Thanksgiving.

Jan. 6, 2001 An auction of Three Rivers Stadium items draws about 9,000 fans to the arena.

Feb. 2, 2001 Alan Jackson

Feb. 8, 2001 Backstreet Boys opens two consecutive concerts.

March 9, 2001 Matchbox 20

March 24, 2001 The NCAA Women's Basketball Tournament East Regional takes place at the arena, sending Connecticut to the Final Four.

Nov. 2, 2001 Britney Spears performs. Later that month, her album *Britney* knocks off Michael Jackson's *Invincible* for the No. 1 spot.

Feb. 18, 2002 Weezer

March 15, 2002 The NCAA Men's Basketball Tournament plays first and second round games.

June 6, 2002 The Historic Review Commission considers historic designation for the arena.

July 31, 2002 A plan seeks $225 million from the state for a new arena. Pittsburgh and Allegheny County say they cannot afford to pay anything.

Aug. 15, 2002 Bow Wow

Nov. 22, 2002 Guns N' Roses

April 26, 2003 Pearl Jam

April 28, 2003 50 Cent

July 15, 2003 *American Idols Live*, featuring nine of the top 11 contestants from the second season of American Idol, appears at the arena. The Idols tour becomes an annual event.

July 28, 2003 Christina Aguilera and Justin Timberlake perform on their *Justified/Stripped* tour.

Feb. 27, 2003 City Council rejects the historic designation for the arena

Aug. 15, 2003 The Wiggles, an Australian singing group for children, opens the first of two shows at the arena and becomes an annual draw.

Sept. 29, 2003 Shania Twain

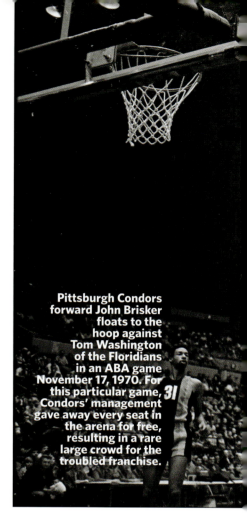

Pittsburgh Condors forward John Brisker floats to the hoop against Tom Washington of the Floridians in an ABA game November 17, 1970. For this particular game, Condors' management gave away every seat in the arena for free, resulting in a rare large crowd for the troubled franchise.

The October 29, 1993, NBA preseason game between the Chicago Bulls and Philadelphia 76ers was one of 25 NBA games played at the arena.

Coppin State players leave the court after a 78-65 upset over No. 2 South Carolina in the 1997 East Regional NCAA tournament game.

CHAZ PALLA

Duquesne University's Eric Evans is fouled by the University of Pittsburgh's Travon Woodall and Brad Wanamaker during the second half of the final City Game at the arena. CHRISTOPHER HORNER

ARTHUR HUNDHAUSEN · REMEMBER THE ABA.COM

BASKETBALL

Championships at the high school, college and professional levels were decided at the arena, but the first game was a regular season Duquesne University victory against Carnegie Tech, 78-40, on December 6, 1961.

Nearly a half-century and many memories later, Duquesne played the last basketball game at the arena December 2, 2009, losing to the University of Pittsburgh, 67-58, in the 35th renewal of the City Game. That's if you don't count one of many Harlem Globetrotter exhibitions, the last of which was staged December 26, 2009.

One of the most memorable games in arena history was held in the first round of the 1997 NCAA Tournament when 18.5-point underdog Coppin State, a tiny school from Baltimore, stunned No. 2 seed South Carolina, 78-65. It was only the third time a No. 15 seed won a game in the tournament.

The Pittsburgh Pipers captured the only pro basketball title at the arena, defeating the New Orleans Buccaneers, 122-113, on May 4, 1968, in the seventh and deciding game of the American Basketball Association championship series.

The NBA played 25 pre-season and regular-season games at the arena from 1973-2006. The last three featured LeBron James and the Cleveland Cavaliers, but James had been there before with his St. Vincent-St. Mary High School team during the 2002-03 season. Another famous prep star, Shaquille O'Neal, played in the 1989 Roundball Classic.

The WPIAL held its championship games at the arena until 1984, starting on March 12, 1963, when a sellout crowd of 10,718 watched Norwin High School and 6-foot-9, 280-pound "Big" John Naponick defeat Aliquippa, 69-64. Schenley (1966), Midland (1971) and Valley (1979) boys team and the Franklin Regional girls ('79) won state titles at the arena.

November 18, 1967
Joan Westin (38) a.k.a. *The Blonde Bomber* who skated for the Bay Bombers was the highest-paid female athlete in the 1960s and '70s.

H.J. HEINZ COLLECTION · HEINZ HISTORY CENTER ARCHIVES

The Arena Football league debuted at the arena on June 19, 1987, and the league's first ArenaBowl was played on August 1, 1987. The Pittsburgh Gladiators lost to the Denver Dynamite, 45-16 in front of 13,232 fans. JAMES M. KUBUS

The Pittsburgh Spirit was one of the original six teams in the Major Indoor Soccer League. The 1983-84 season was their best with a 32-16 record. JAMES M. KUBUS

Dec. 23, 2003 The Trans-Siberian Orchestra brings its hard rock-metal Christmas show to the arena for the first time, starting an annual tradition.

Jan. 8, 2004 Bette Midler

March 3, 2004 Rod Stewart

June 16, 2004 Simon & Garfunkel

Oct. 6, 2004 Usher

April 23, 2005 Green Day

July 20, 2005 Destiny's Child

July 29, 2005 The Bassmaster Classic fishing tournament comes to Pittsburgh, holding its weigh-in ceremonies at the arena. Michigan's Kevin VanDam wins, setting a record for the lowest winning weight.

Oct. 30, 2005 The Xplosion play their first ABA game at the arena. The franchise lasts three seasons.

Dec. 21, 2005 The Penguins unveil plans to build a new arena with money from an adjacent casino. The deal hinges on Isle of Capri Casinos winning the license for a Pittsburgh slots parlor.

March 30, 2006 Governor Ed Rendell proposes a Plan B for building a new arena with gambling money.

June 29, 2006 Cirque du Soleil opens three days of acrobatic shows.

Sept. 30, 2006 Blue Man Group

Oct. 28, 2006 Comedian Larry the Cable Guy

Dec. 17, 2006 The Cheetah Girls

Jan. 6, 2007 Disney's *High School Musical on Ice* plays at the arena.

Feb. 16, 2007 George Strait with Ronnie Milsap and Taylor Swift

March 19, 2007 Justin Timberlake with Pink

April 14, 2007 Christina Aguilera with Danity Kane and the Pussycat Dolls

Aug. 4, 2007 Josh Groban performs at the arena. He attended Carnegie Mellon University briefly before being offered a recording contract.

Nov. 9, 2007 Stevie Wonder performs his second and final show at the arena. He first played at the arena in 1980.

Nov. 11, 2007 Keith Urban with Gary Allan

Jan. 4, 2008 Miley Cyrus with the Jonas Brothers

March 13, 2008 The Reverend Joel Osteen draws thousands to a religious service.

In 1990 the Pittsburgh Bulls were a professional team in the Major Indoor Lacrosse League and lasted until 1994. Then, in 2000, the Baltimore franchise in the National Lacrosse League relocated to Pittsburgh, and became the CrosseFire but lasted only one season before moving to Washington.

U.S. Olympic gold medalist Bart Conner on the 1984 American champions gymnastic tour.

CHAZ PALLA

There were 11,000 fans were on hand to visit the Water Show that featured professional divers, synchronized swimmers and water races in July 1962.

MELLON ARENA

SINGING AND SWINGING
CHAPTER SEVEN

F ROM CIVIC ARENA'S EARLIEST DAYS, IT ATTRACTED THE BEST ACTS IN THE WORLD.

The Ice Capades, the creation of Pittsburgh entertainment entrepreneur John Harris, opened the arena on September 19, 1961. The building's very first concert, exactly a month later, was given by Judy Garland.

What a place the brand-new arena was, said promoter Pete Bennett, who worked with the Beatles, the Rolling Stones and Frank Sinatra. He booked Nat King Cole at the arena in 1963, and remembered those days as "an exciting time."

Sinatra appeared at the arena eight times, and the famous maestro, Leonard Bernstein, but once. He complained about the acoustics.

When the circus came to town, wild animals were kept in the arena's lower-level convention center space, which worked fine until the elephants figured out how to pull the fire alarms, setting them off several times before anyone identified the culprits. Giraffes, meanwhile, were kept outside and helped themselves to the leaves on nearby trees.

Madonna insisted stagehands turn their backs when she entered the building in 1985. And an argument between Stephen Stills and David Crosby of Crosby, Stills & Nash spilled onto the stage in 1982.

The Beatles arrived at the arena on September 14, 1964, carrying their own instruments. Kids had been hiding in bathrooms and closets throughout the building, hoping to catch a glimpse of the Fab Four.

From a transcript of the press conference before the arena performance:

Q: "Gentlemen, I would like your reaction to the Civic Arena in which we're located. Did you see the outside?"

BEATLES: "Yeah!"

GEORGE: "Is this the place that can be changed into an open-air?"

Q: "The roof opens up."

JOHN: "Very good. Good idea, that. I hope they don't lift the roof while we're playing."

(reporters chuckle)

PAUL: "So do I."

JAMES M. KUBUS

Ray Charles (1968)
WALT HARPER ARCHIVES

Kenny Rogers (1983)
JAMES M. KUBUS

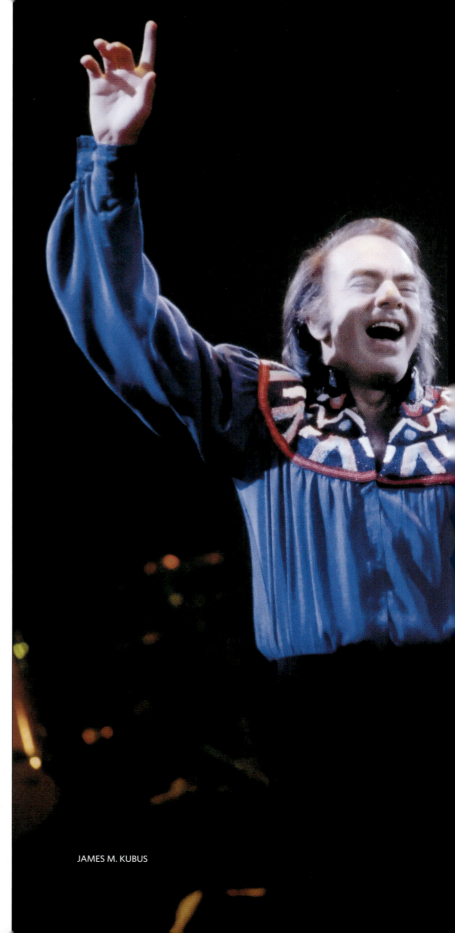
JAMES M. KUBUS

NEIL DIAMOND

had a record 18 shows at the arena from 1971 to 2008. Here are the dates:

Oct. 8, 1971
Oct. 20, 1976
Dec. 8, 1978
June 7, 1982
June 8, 1982
Feb. 14, 1984
Feb. 15, 1984
April 7, 1986
April 8, 1986
Jan. 29, 1989
Jan. 30, 1989
March 1, 1992
March 2, 1992
June 25, 1996
June 26, 1996
Feb. 16, 2002
Aug. 26, 2005
Aug. 18, 2008

The Beatles (1964)
JOHN DUNLAP

The Beach Boys (1974)
WILLIAM LOEFFLER

Iron Maiden (1988)
STEVE KALINSKY

ZZ Top (1984)
JAMES M. KUBUS

Metallica (1989)

Bon Jovi (2005)
ANDREW RUSSELL

Marilyn Manson (1999)
TRIB TOTAL MEDIA ARCHIVES

The Police (1983) RICH MALKIN

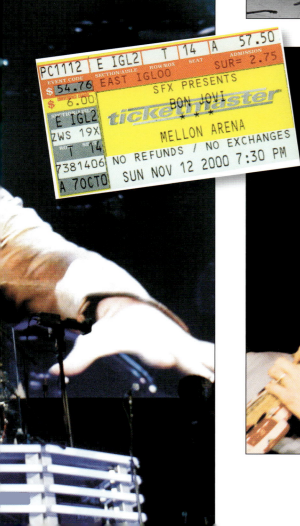

Van Halen
HEINZ HISTORY CENTER ARCHIVES

Cyndi Lauper (1984)
RICH MALKIN

Tina Turner (2000)
STEVE KALINSKY

Christina Aguilera (2007)
ANDREW RUSSELL

Celine Dion (1997)

Dionne Warwick (1984)
JAMES M. KUBUS

Paula Abdul (1990)
STEVE KALINSKY

Madonna (1985)
STEVE KALINSKY

Faith Hill (2007)

Janet Jackson (2001)
STEVE KALINSKY

Sammy Davis Jr. and Frank Sinatra (1988)
Dean Martin cancels due to illness.
STEVE KALINSKY

Stevie Wonder (1997)
JASON NELSON

U2 (2001)
J.C. SCHISLER

Michael Jackson (1988)
JAMES M. KUBUS

AEROSMITH (1990) STEVE KALINSKY

KISS (2009) STEVE KALINSKY

AC/DC (2008) JOE APPEL

Rod Stewart (1988)
STEVE KALINSKY

Garth Brooks (1997)
JOE APPEL

Paul McCartney (1990)
JAMES M. KUBUS

Prince (1997)

Eric Clapton (1992)
STEVE KALINSKY

Jerry Garcia of The Grateful Dead (1985) STEVE KALINSKY

Bruce Springsteen (2009) STEVE KALINSKY

Rush (1996)

Queensrÿche (1988) STEVE KALINSKY

Crosby, Stills, Nash and Young (2000) KEITH HODAN

Joe Grushecky with Rusted Root lead singer Michael Glabiki (2005) ANDREW RUSSELL

Robert Plant and Jimmy Page (1998) PHILIP G. PAVELY

Fleetwood Mac (2009) JOE APPEL

The Jonas Brothers (2009) STEVE KALINSKY

Genesis (1984)

World's Largest Orchestra (1998)

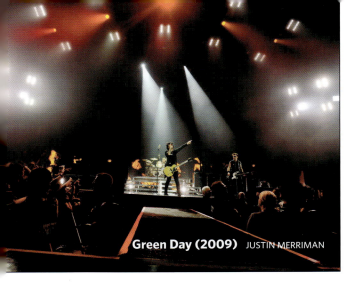
Green Day (2009) JUSTIN MERRIMAN

***NSYNC (1999)**

Jesus Christ Superstar (1971)
MELLON ARENA

May 17, 2008 Hank Williams Jr. and Lynyrd Skynyrd

Sept. 13, 2008 Ventriloquist and stand-up comedian Jeff Dunham

Oct. 17, 2008 Reba McEntire and Kelly Clarkson

Oct. 27, 2008 Democratic presidential candidate Barack Obama draws about 15,800 to the arena for a rally. He wins the general election a week later.

May 7, 2009 Comedian Dane Cook

June 2, 2009 The Penguins play the Detroit Red Wings in a Stanley Cup Final game. Pittsburgh wins its third championship, in Game 7 on the road.

Oct. 1, 2009 Taylor Swift with Gloriana and Kellie Pickler

Oct. 11, 2009 Filming of *Love and Other Drugs* starts at the arena.

Nov. 29, 2009 *Star Wars in Concert* plays at the arena with a multimedia show set to a live orchestra performance.

March 4, 2010 Black Eyed Peas with LMFAO and Ludacris

March 16, 2010 Jay-Z with Trey Songz and Young Jeezy

April 1, 2010 The Pennsylvania Interscholastic Hockey League holds its final championship game at the arena, with Mars defeating West Chester Rustin, 4-1, in Class A.

April 8, 2010 The Penguins play their final regular-season game, winning 7-3 over the New York Islanders.

April 14, 2010 The Penguins open the first round of the 2010 Stanley Cup Playoffs. They lose 5-4 to the Ottawa Senators, but go on to win the series 4-2.

April 11, 2010 The Shrine Circus, the final circus to perform at the arena, closes six shows in three days.

May 10, 2010 WWE Raw presents the final professional wrestling event at the arena.

May 12, 2010 The Penguins play their final game at the arena, a 5-2 playoff loss to the Montreal Canadiens.

June 26, 2010 The arena's final concert features James Taylor and Carole King. They first played together at the arena in 1971.

August 1, 2010 The building becomes the Civic Arena once again when the naming rights contract expires, and the Penguins leave for the new CONSOL Energy Center, Uptown.

Ringling Brothers and Barnum & Bailey Circus (1995)
MICHAEL HARITAN

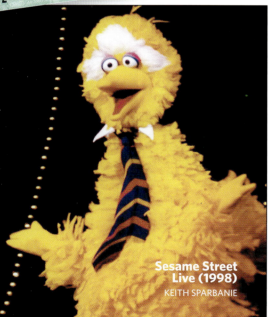

Sesame Street Live (1998)
KEITH SPARBANIE

Harlem Globetrotters (1996)

U.S. Hot Rod Thundernationals (1997)
MICHAEL HARITAN

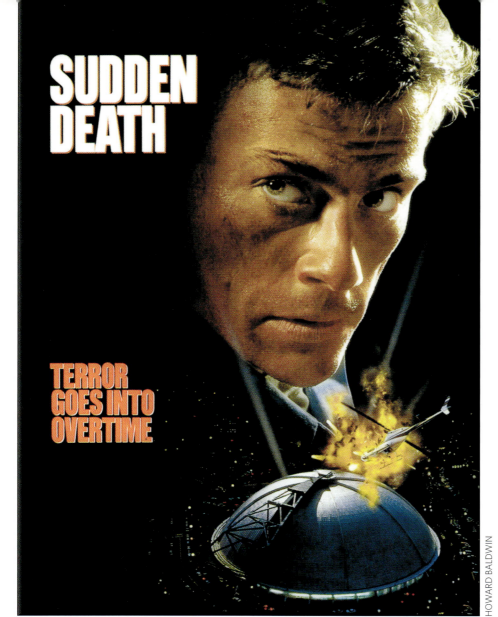

Several movies have been shot at the Civic Arena. But it got the most screen time in *Sudden Death*, a 1995 action movie starring Jean-Claude Van Damme as a Pittsburgh firefighter who takes his kids to Game 7 of the Stanley Cup Final and gets caught in a terrorist plot. *Sudden Death* was written by Karen Elise Baldwin, wife of then-Penguins owner Harold Baldwin. It was shot during the 1994-95 National Hockey League lockout. Other movies with an arena flavor are: *The Fish that Saved Pittsburgh*, pictured above (1979); *Zack and Miri Make a Porno* (2008); *She's Out of My League*, pictured left (2010); and *Love and Other Drugs* (2010).

April 10, 1966
About 3,000 worshipers were chilled when all six of the arena roof leaves were retracted shortly after 6 a.m. for Easter Sunrise Services. CLYDE HARE ARCHIVE

CELEBRATIONS
CHAPTER EIGHT

WITH MAGENTA STREAMERS DRAPED OVER ITS SCOREBOARD, the Civic Arena served as a "temple for the glory of God," in the words of then-Bishop Donald Wuerl, when the Catholic Diocese of Pittsburgh celebrated its 150th anniversary in 1993.

That was just one of many days when the public auditorium was transformed for Masses, revivals and national religious conferences. In the early years, Roman Catholics regularly celebrated Labor Day Masses there, and Protestants came to worship on Easter mornings.

In 1964, the nation's civil rights debate came to the arena when 800 angry Methodists knelt in prayer outside the church's General Conference to protest racial segregation.

American Baptists, Southern Baptists and Jehovah's Witnesses held national conventions there. The Byzantine Catholic Diocese of Pittsburgh celebrated its 50th anniversary at the arena in 1974, and Roman Catholics gathered to honor the Black Madonna of Poland in 1982.

The Rev. Jimmy Swaggart brought his Evangelical Crusade to the arena in the 1980s; Promise Keepers met there in 1995; and the Rev. Joel Osteen filled the building with his followers in 2008.

But celebrations weren't just spiritual. The arena hosted boisterous rallies for political candidates and joyful commencement ceremonies for high schools and colleges. Some grads remember shivering through the ceremonies because surface ice still was needed for Penguins games or ice shows and merely had been covered over.

About 800 attendees of the General Conference of the Methodist Church hold a kneel-in to protest church segregation on May 2, 1964.

MISSION EDUCATION COLLECTION, GENERAL COMMISSION ON ARCHIVES AND HISTORY, THE UNITED METHODIST CHURCH, MADISON, NEW JERSEY.

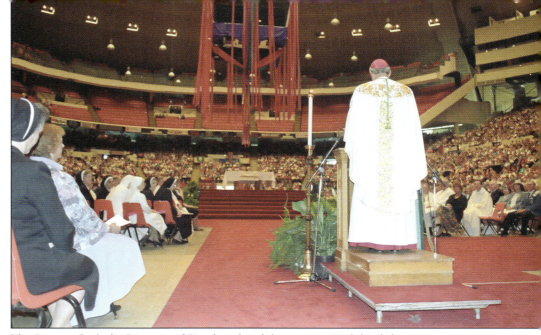

The Roman Catholic Diocese of Pittsburgh celebrates its 150th birthday September 19, 1993. TRIB TOTAL MEDIA ARCHIVES

Inclement weather kept the dome closed for the Protestant Easter Sunrise Service on March 29, 1964.
CLYDE HARE ARCHIVE

Pittsburgh Peabody High School class of 1974   RICH MALKIN

Duquesne University graduation, May 31, 1964.   BOB RATHKE

The last high school commencement at the arena was that of Pittsburgh Langley High School's class of 2010. PHILIP G. PAVELY

Point Park University graduation 2010   KEITH HODAN

ON THE STUMP

It never hosted a presidential nominating convention, but the arena helped launch presidential candidates to victory.

Lyndon Johnson touted his Great Society to thousands during a campaign speech in 1964 that contained references to David L. Lawrence, Abraham Lincoln and John F. Kennedy. Johnson, a Democrat, would go on win a term as president.

Republican Richard Nixon drew some 17,000 people to a rally on October 28, 1968, just days before sweeping into office amid a turbulent election year. In a bid for labor votes even in a heavily Democratic city, Nixon promised support for the steel industry and met with John J. Wright, then-Bishop of the Roman Catholic Diocese of Pittsburgh, before leaving town. Still, Nixon failed to carry Pennsylvania.

A generation later, Democrat Barack Obama rallied supporters a week before winning the White House. On October 27, 2008, Obama brought his message of change to the arena and promised the crowd of about 15,800 a middle-class tax cut. He carried Pennsylvania when he won the election a week later.

PHILIP G. PAVELY

Former President Dwight D. Eisenhower jubilantly responds to roughly 17,000 people cramming the Civic Arena on October 25, 1962. Eisenhower was stumping for Republican candidates in the November election. He appealed to Americans to make whatever personal sacrifices were necessary during the Cuban missile crisis, but criticized President John F. Kennedy, a Democrat, on domestic issues. TEENIE HARRIS · CARNEGIE MUSEUM OF ART

Thousands of people waited for hours to hear President Lyndon Johnson deliver a campaign speech at the Civic Arena on October 27, 1964. He told them: "And as I came into this magnificent building tonight, and I saw the new Pittsburgh, and I saw all of these happy, smiling faces I just wished that everybody in our country could be here, because I think it would be contagious." One week later, Johnson, a Democrat, defeated Republican Barry Goldwater in the general election. TEENIE HARRIS · CARNEGIE MUSEUM OF ART

The dome of the Civic Arena is reflected in the windows of the CONSOL Energy Center, which is set to open August 18, 2010, with a concert by Paul McCartney.
KEITH HODAN

ACKNOWLEDGEMENTS

THIS BOOK – A TRIBUTE TO AN ICONIC BUILDING IN A CITY RICH WITH UNIQUE, MEMORABLE, MASTERFUL AND HISTORIC STRUCTURES – RESULTS FROM THE EFFORTS OF MANY INDIVIDUALS AND INSTITUTIONS.

We are grateful for the support and guidance of all of them, including:

- Jay Roberts, Rob Goodman and Alyssa Blumming from SMG, for access to their arena event database;
- S. Philip Hundley, principal at DRS Architects, who provided images, internal correspondence and documents dating to the days when the firm's founding partners, James A. Mitchell and Dahlen K. Ritchey, designed the arena and laid out a sweeping master plan for the city in 1947;
- Martin Aurand, architectural librarian at Carnegie Mellon University, archivist of the university's Architecture Archives and head of its Arts Library and Special Collections, who provided architectural drawings, original documents and historic photographs from the arena's planning, construction and earliest days;
- Pittsburgh Penguins President David Morehouse and Tom McMillan, Penguins vice-president of communications, who gave their blessing to this project;
- the staff of the Senator John Heinz History Center, and particularly to Andy Masich, the center's president and CEO; Ned Schano, its communications director; Robert Stakeley, archivist; and C. Art Louderback, chief librarian, who provided insight, original source documents and photographs from the arena's planning and development;
- Kristin Archbold, communications specialist with the Pittsburgh Civic Light Opera, who offered guidance and context on the opera company's history.

In addition, I offer my personal thanks to the Pittsburgh Tribune-Review's reporters, photographers, artists, editors and other staff who contributed to or supported *Inside the Igloo*.

In particular, without the invaluable vision, unwavering commitment and tireless work of Trib staffers James Kubus, Andrew Conte, Elizabeth Kane Jackson, Carol Shrefler and Sandra Skowron, this book would not have been conceived, written, edited, designed or produced.

FRANK L. CRAIG
Editor of the Pittsburgh Tribune-Review

REFERENCES & SOURCES

Alcoa Corporation

The American Presidency Project

The Associated Press

Marty Allen

Archive Service Center, University of Pittsburgh
With special thanks to
Miriam Meislik, media curator, and Wendy Pflug, reference archivist

Bank of New York Mellon Corporation

Pete Bennett

Bill Blakey

Dan Bylsma

Carnegie Library of Pittsburgh, Pennsylvania Department

Carnegie Mellon University Architecture Archives
With special thanks to
Architecture Librarian and Archivist Martin Aurand, head of the Arts Library and Special Collections department

Lauretta Comans

Edna Council

Sidney Crosby

John DeFazio

DRS Architects
With special thanks to
S. Philip Hundley, principal

Sandy Duncan

Rich Engler

Don't Call Me Boss: David L. Lawrence, Pittsburgh's Renaissance Mayor, by Michael P. Weber, University of Pittsburgh Press, 1988

Forging the Pittsburgh Renaissance: Urban Redevelopment Authority of Pittsburgh Fifty Years, by Bessie C. Economou, Urban Redevelopment Authority of Pittsburgh, 1997

Frediani Printing

William J. Gaughan Collection, Archives Service Center, University of Pittsburgh

Senator John Heinz History Center
With special thanks to
Andy Masich, president and CEO; Ned Schano, director of communications; C. Art Louderback, chief librarian; Robert Stakeley, archivist

Elaine Heufelder

Hill District Consensus Group

Hockey Hall of Fame
With special thanks to
Miragh Bitove, archivist and collections registrar

James M. Kubus

Lorimar Productions Inc.

Lowell MacDonald

Jay McKee

John Menniti, architect

Merchant Prince and Master Builder: Edgar Kaufmann and Frank Lloyd Wright, by Richard Cleary, The Heinz Architectural Center, 1999

National Council of Jewish Women Oral History Project

Lenora Nemetz

Brooks Orpik

Robert Pease

Penn State University Libraries

The Pennsylvania Center for the Book – Mellon Arena, Penn State University

Pfaffmann + Associates
With special thanks to
Rob Pfaffmann, principal

Frank Pietrangelo

Pittsburgh Civic Light Opera
With special thanks to
Kristin Archbold, communications specialist

Pittsburgh Civic Light Opera: How the Dreams Came True, by Mary Brignano, White Oak Publishing, 1996

Pittsburgh City Planning Commission Records, 1928-1962, Archives Service Center, University of Pittsburgh

Pittsburgh Film Office
With special thanks to
Dawn Keezer, director

Pittsburgh History & Landmarks Foundation

PittsburghHockey.net

Pittsburgh Penguins
With special thanks to
David Morehouse, president, and Tom McMillan, vice president of communications

Pittsburgh Tribune-Review

Preservation Pittsburgh

Carl Redwood

Audrey & Chuck Reichblum

Reuse the Igloo!

Jack Riley

Chita Rivera

Duane Rupp

Richard M. Scaife

Ken Schinkel

SMG
With special thanks to
Jay Roberts, general manager; Rob Goodman, assistant general manager & director of marketing and Alyssa Blumming, assistant marketing manager

Sports & Exhibition Authority of Pittsburgh and Allegheny County
With special thanks to
Mary Conturo, executive director

Sridhar Seetharaman, Professor of Materials Science and Engineering, Carnegie Mellon University

Jordan Staal

Max Talbot

Teenie Harris Collection, Carnegie Museum of Art, Pittsburgh

Thomas Mellon and His Times, by Thomas Mellon, University of Pittsburgh Press, 1996

United States Patent Office

United States Steel Corporation

George Von Benko

Warner Bros. Entertainment Inc.

Michael P. Weber Papers, 1963-1984, Archives Service Center, University of Pittsburgh

Abraham L. Wolk Papers, 1937-1963, Archives Service Center, University of Pittsburgh

Elliott Wolk

Western Pennsylvania Conservancy

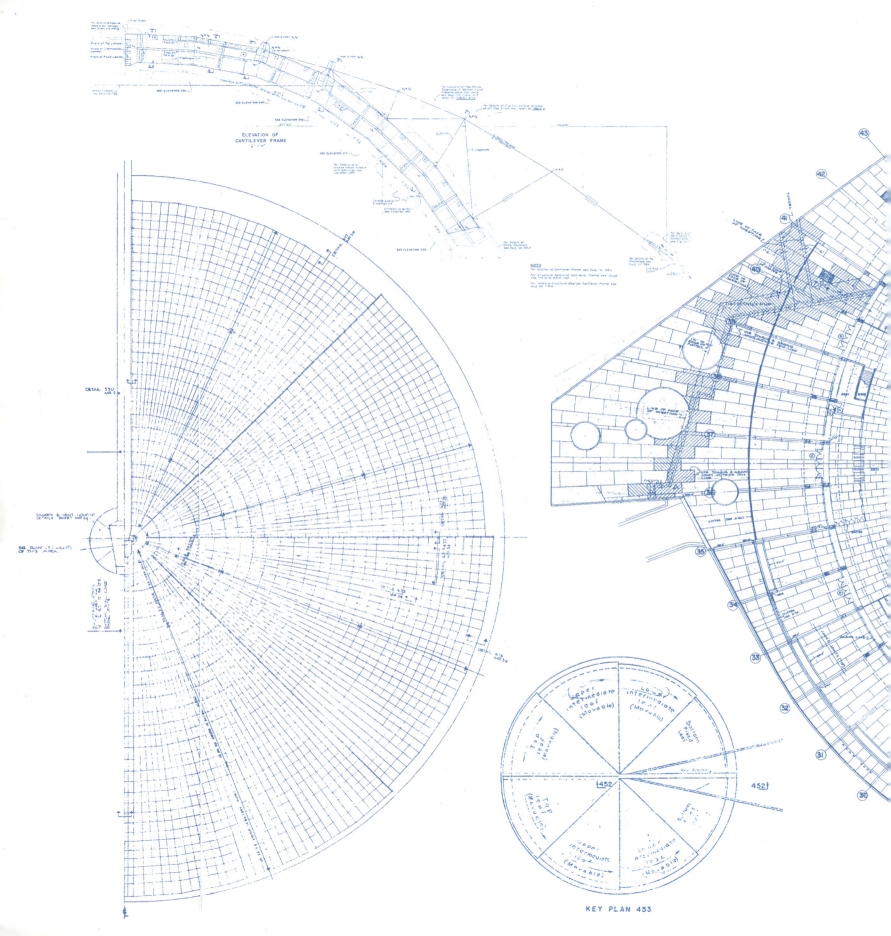